PHOTOGRAPHY made easy

Other titles in this series:

MOTORBIKE mechanics
YOUR CAR fault finder
What to FREEZE and how
YOGA for you
How to play TENNIS

PHOTOGRAPHY made easy

Text by Roy Green
Illustrations by P. Dupuis
Series editor P. Cassidy

Mirror Books

Published by Mirror Books Ltd.,
Athene House, 66/73 Shoe Lane,
London EC4P 4AB
for Mirror Group Newspapers Ltd.

This Paperback edition June 1980

Produced for Mirror Books Ltd by
Chancerel Publishers Ltd.,
40 Tavistock Street,
London WC2E 7PB.

ISBN 0 85939 211 2

Origination by ReproSharp, London EC1.

Printed in Great Britain by
Richard Clay (The Chaucer Press) Ltd.,
Bungay, Suffolk, England.

CONTENTS

Chapter 1	Introducing photography	7
Chapter 2	Choosing a camera	11
Chapter 3	The essential controls	17
Chapter 4	Choosing a film	28
Chapter 5	All kinds of lenses	35
Chapter 6	Coping from the start	45
Chapter 7	Taking pictures indoors	55
Chapter 8	Natural pictures outdoors	64
Chapter 9	On holiday	72
Chapter 10	Photos — anytime, anywhere	85
Chapter 11	Photo action	95
Chapter 12	Altering the image	100
Chapter 13	Film processing	106
Chapter 14	Making prints	114
Chapter 15	Something to show	119

Chapter 1

INTRODUCING PHOTOGRAPHY

In just over 150 years the camera has revolutionised our way of looking at the world. From snapshots to television, pictures allow people all around the world to see and understand ideas and events immediately. On an individual level, photography is one of the most popular and absorbing leisure interests, giving a personal record of people, places and events.

Despite the apparent gulf between the large, old-fashioned mahogany and brass plate apparatus and the latest, sleek, microcomputer-controlled 35mm camera, the basic concept of photography is still the same. The subject in front of the camera is caught on light-sensitive material — film. By means of a chemical reaction the image on the film is revealed and used to print a picture.

Here are some of the major milestones in photographic history, with approximate dates:

1822 In France, Nicephore Niépce took the world's first photograph. It was not possible to reproduce from it.
1835 William Henry Fox Talbot and Louis Jacques Mande Daguerre, working separately, both evolved a negative-positive process.
1840 Josef Petzval designed a fast (f/3.6) lens which made photography really practicable.
1861 Sir James Clerk-Maxwell demonstrated that colour photography was feasible.
1869 Louis Ducos du Hauron took the world's first colour photograph in France.
1888 George Eastman brought photography to the masses with the launch of the Kodak roll-film camera.
1925 Oskar Barnack produced the Leica, the camera which really launched today's 35mm photography.
1935 Launch of Kodachrome, the first practical colour slide film.
1936 The Exakta, the first single lens reflex (SLR) 35mm camera.
1949 First pentaprism SLR, giving right-way round, easy-focus viewing: the Contax S.
1969 First auto-exposure 35mm SLR, the Konica Autoreflex T.

Between these major strides in camera development, there are many thousands of detailed improvements, and cameras are still being improved. As a result modern miniature cameras, especially the 35mm SLR, enable anyone to master quickly the basic technical necessities and concentrate on taking good pictures.

How it all began

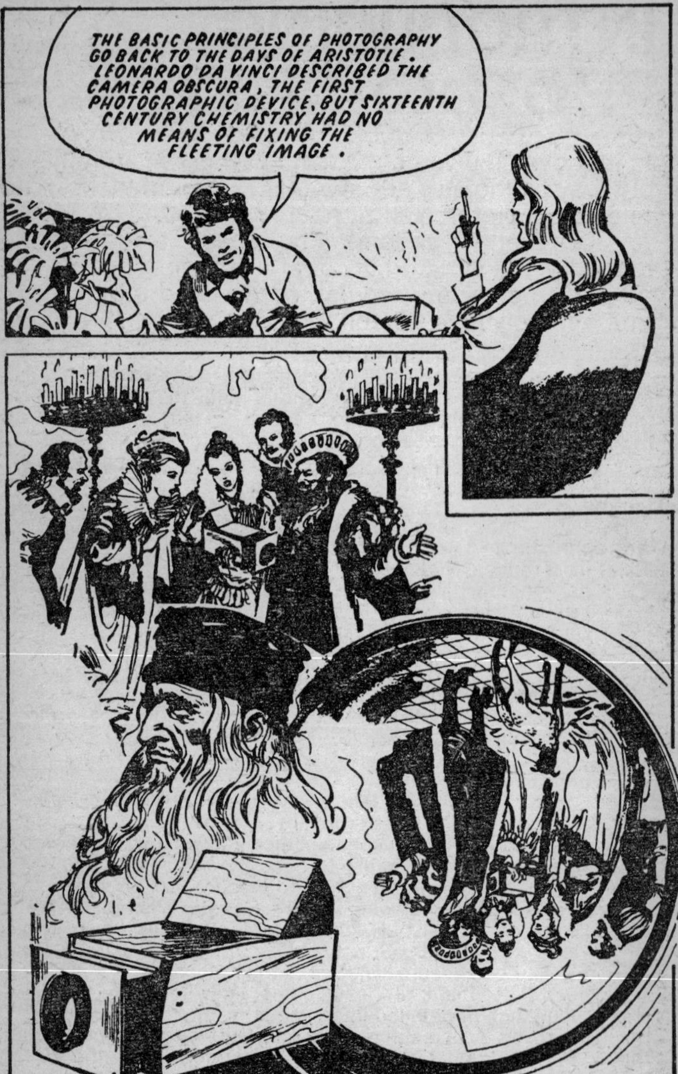

Fixing the image

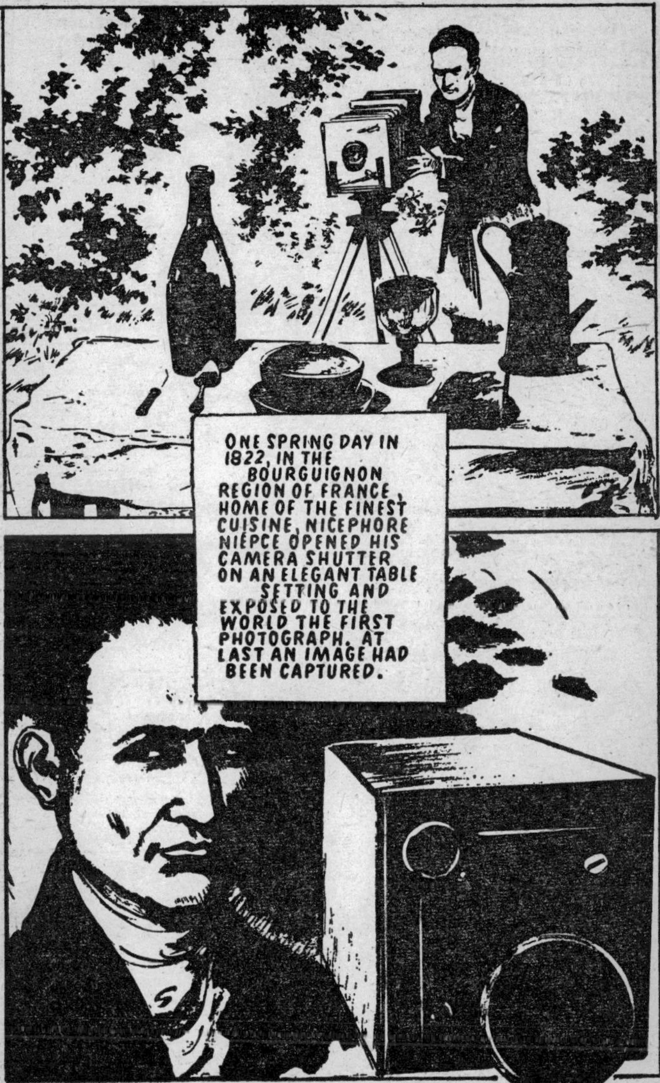

The age of invention

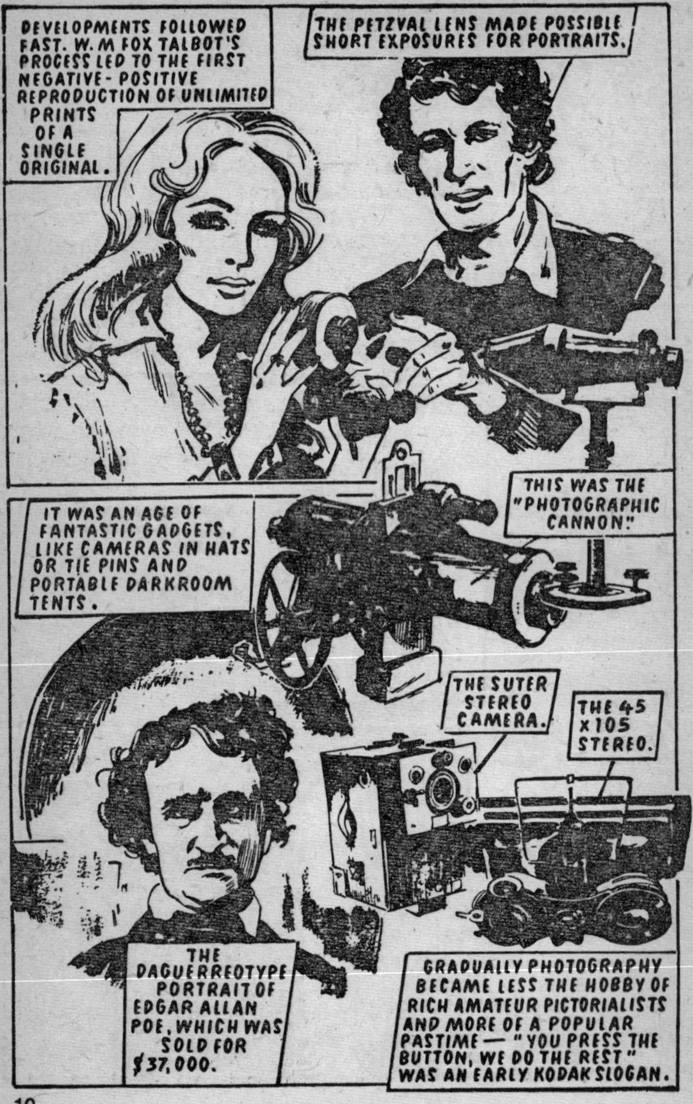

Chapter 2

CHOOSING A CAMERA

Which type of camera is best? How much will a good camera cost? Will a tiny cartridge camera really give good pictures? Will it take colour? These are the common questions asked by prospective camera buyers. And, apart from the last one, they're sticky questions to answer until the would-be photographer thinks harder about his or her intentions and ambitions. As for colour, most cameras on the market will take colour film and give acceptable pictures in good light, or indoors with the aid of flash. For an overall picture of camera choice, here's a guide to the main types, their advantages and limitations.

110 Cartridge

Negative size 13 × 17mm. Number of shots: 12, 20 or 24.

These pocket cameras usually have few controls. They will give negatives producing acceptable small prints in good light conditions, so they are fine for snapshots. Some types have built-in flash units for indoor pictures. Most have fixed focus, so everything is sharp from about 1.2m (4ft), to infinity.

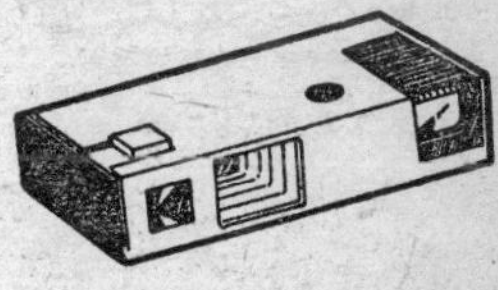

More expensive types have varying exposure settings and sometimes two-lens settings. The best 110 cameras are versatile SLR types but these are expensive, and great care is needed to get results comparable with those from cameras taking larger films.

35mm non reflex camera

Negative size 24 × 36mm. Number of shots: 20, 24 or 36.

Generally more versatile than cartridge types, but still quite small, often called compacts. They give good quality pictures more easily than the 110 because of the larger film size and generally better-quality lenses. If you want a modest-priced camera that will do most of the

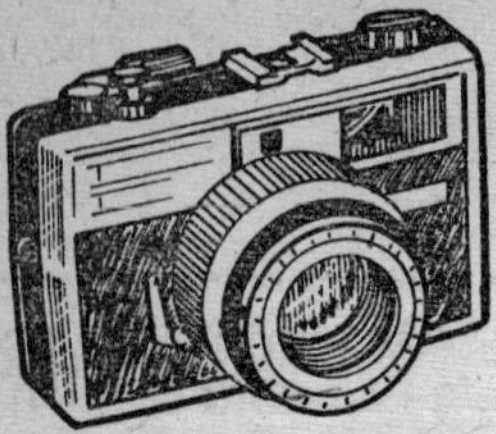

technical thinking, look at this type of camera. Most types handle exposure automatically. Focusing is by rangefinder scale or symbol setting, or automatic. Many models have built-in flash. On a few top-price models lenses can be changed.

35mm single lens reflex (SLR)

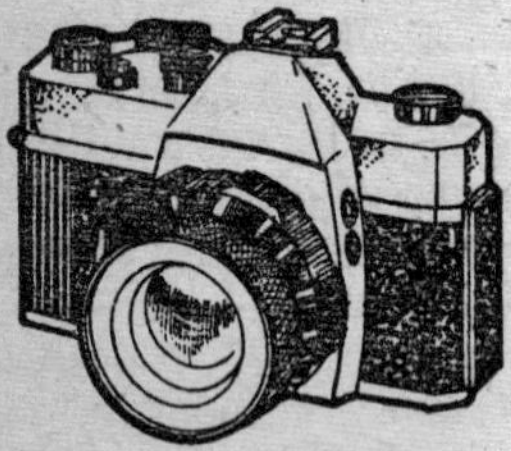

Negative size: 24 × 36mm. Number of shots: 20, 24 or 36.
A truly universal camera with great versatility. It's chief advantage is that the lenses are interchangeable, allowing the camera to take in a very wide view or magnify distant objects to fill the frame. Because viewing is through the taking lens, precise focusing and composing is easy. SLRs can be used with many accessories making them very flexible.

Roll film cameras 2¼ ins. square

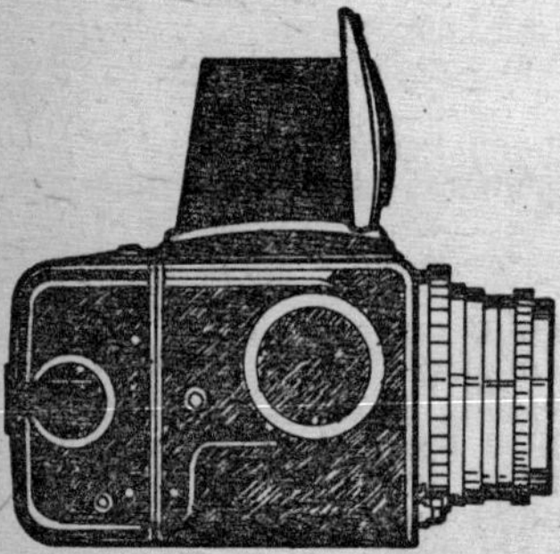

Negative size: 6cm wide × 4.5, 6, 7 or 9cm. Number of shots: 10, 12, 15.

High-quality, and expensive cameras, only really necessary if you require extra-quality large photographs, usually for professional use. The twin-lens reflex is one variation of this type. It is very popular with wedding photographers, who find the larger negative gives good quality enlargements with relative ease.

Pocket cameras at the ready

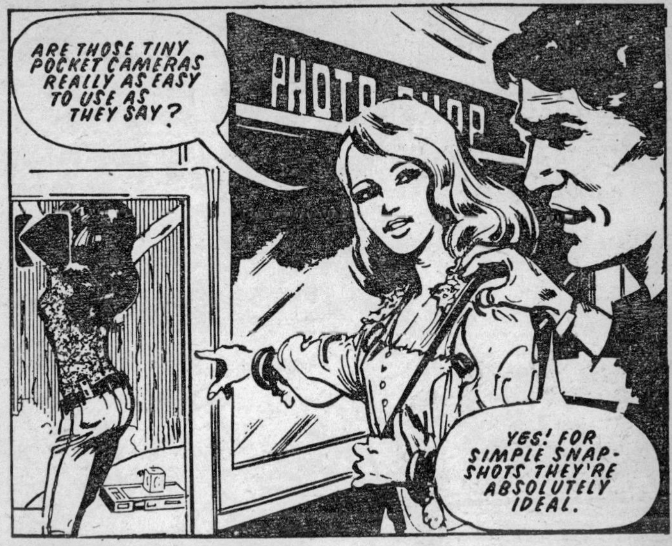

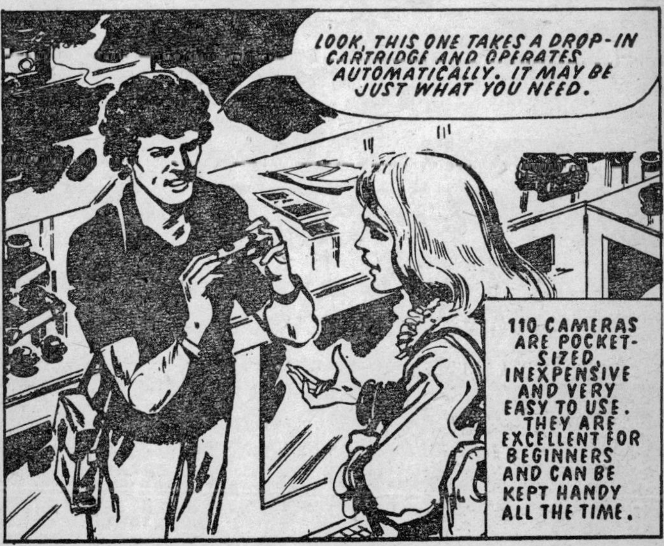

The universal camera

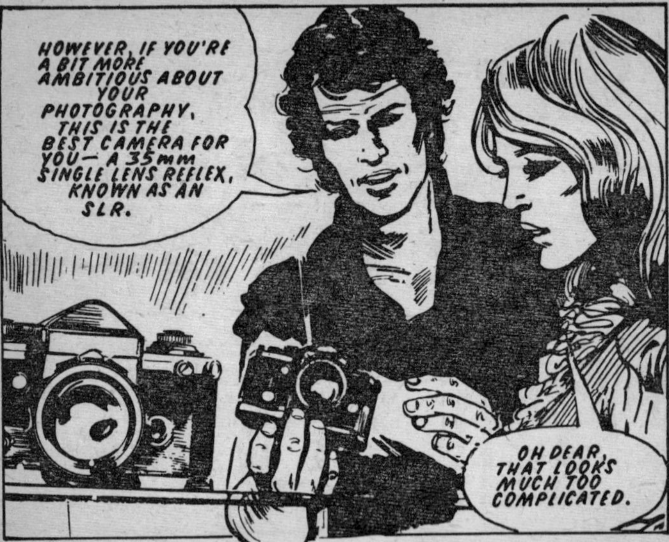

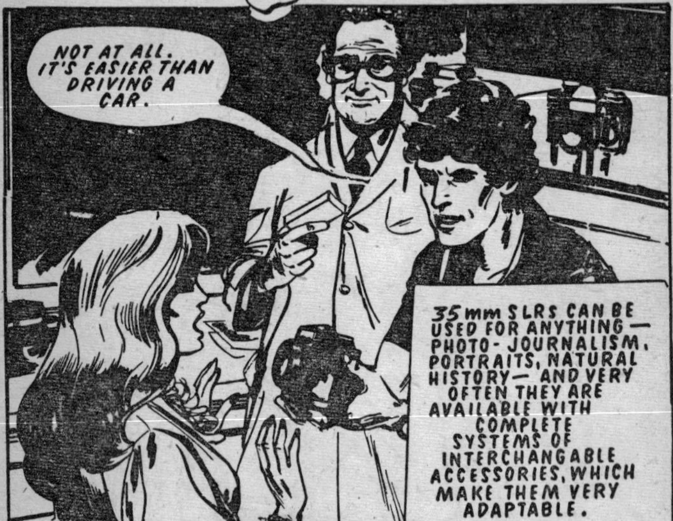

SLR or rangefinder?

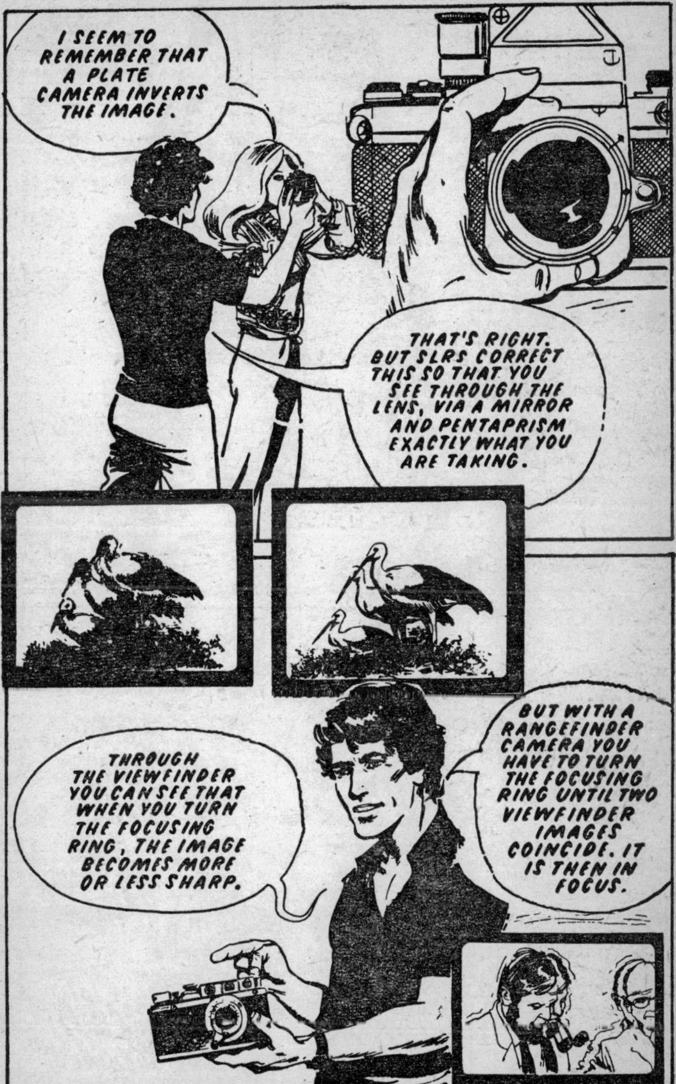

The big league

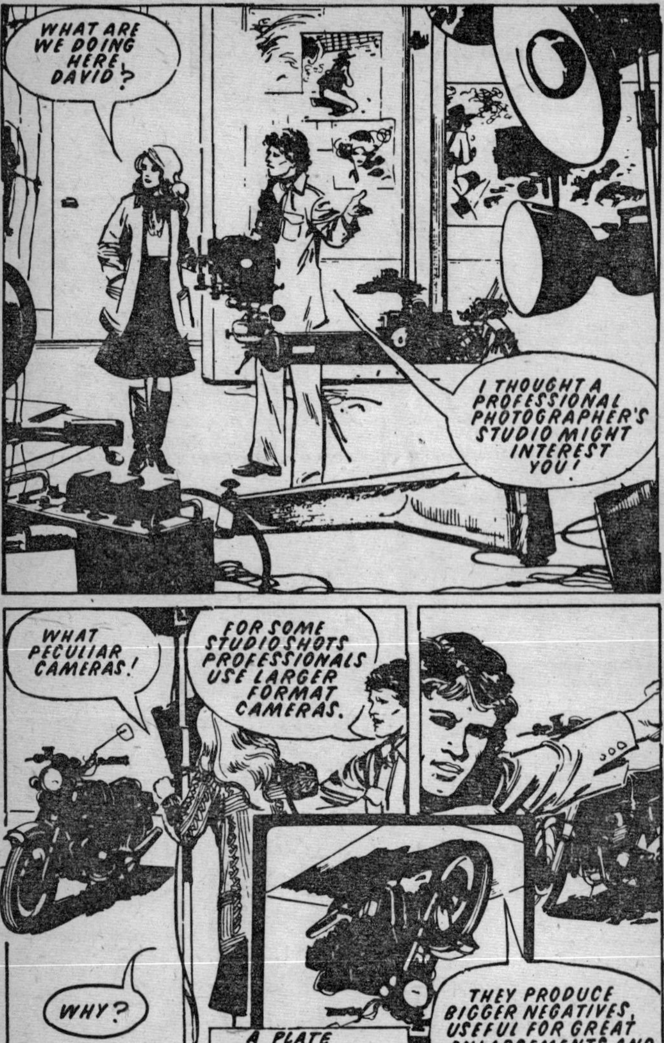

Chapter 3

THE ESSENTIAL CONTROLS

The main camera controls are for assessing the amount of light needed for correct exposure of the film; setting the aperture and shutter speed to suit the exposure; and adjusting the focus. With some cameras you have to handle all these yourself, though many models today have automatic controls. Even so, to control your results you really need to understand some of the key functions.

Measuring the exposure

There are four means of ensuring correct exposure: hand meters, simple meters on the camera, built-in camera metering on SLRs (TTL type), and automatic metering.

Hand-held

Light measurements are taken on the meter and the readings are transferred to camera. Slower than in-camera metering, but very reliable.

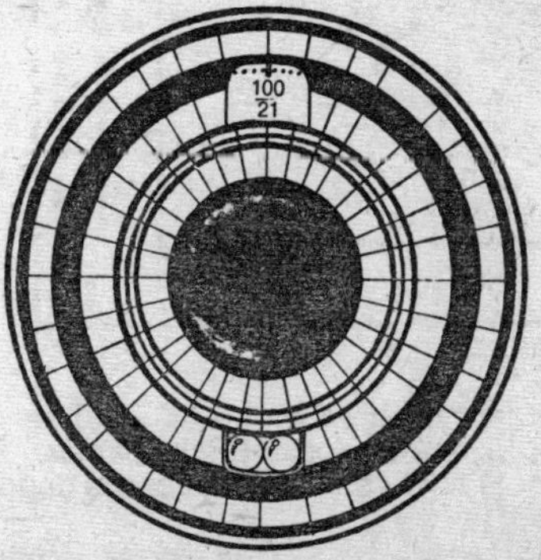

The front view of an in-camera light meter, showing the sensor cell and ASA dial.

In-camera

A sensor cell on the lens or camera reads light strength. Aperture and shutter dial are adjusted to match the meter reading.

TTL (through the lens)

Light from the scene photographed enters an SLR's lens and is read by sensor cells in the camera body. Aperture or shutter speed is adjusted until an indicator seen in the viewfinder shows exposure is correct. Versatile and quite accurate.

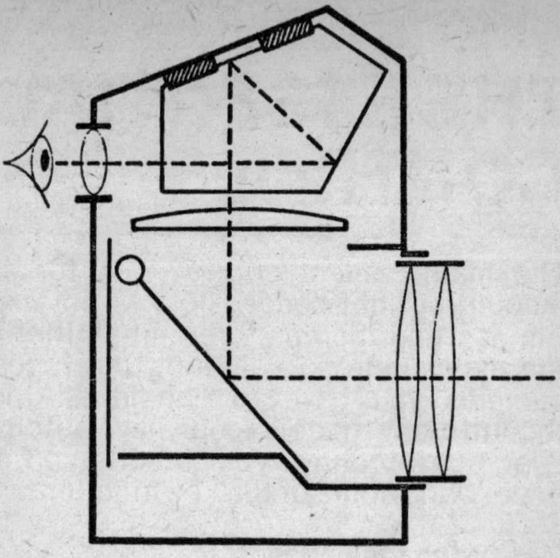

The path of light through an SLR camera. The eye sees the actual scene to be photographed through the lens, via a mirror and pentaprism.

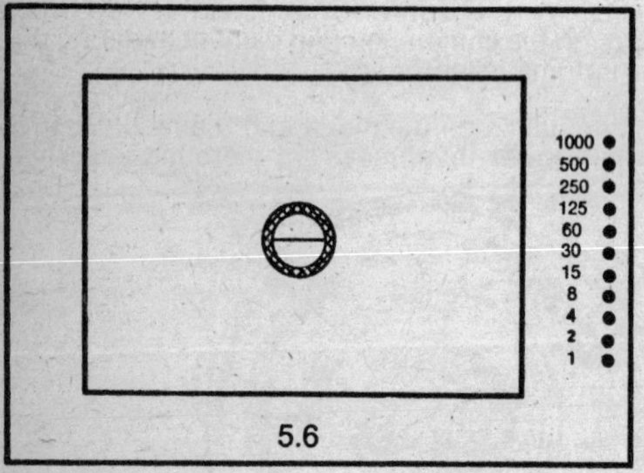

A typical viewfinder layout on a 35mm SLR camera, showing aperture (bottom centre) and shutter speed (right).

Automatic
Light strength is measured by an external sensor cell (on non-reflexes) or TTL meter (on SLRs). Camera electronically or mechanically sets either shutter or aperture or both automatically.

The lens aperture — shutter speed partnership

The aperture range is marked on the lens, as shown here. Typical shutter speeds available on a good-class SLR, ranging in equal steps from 1/1000th sec to 1 sec, are marked on the bottom scale. For a given amount of available light (represented on the diagram by the centre point) a number of combinations will give the same, correct exposure. 1/1000th of a second at f/2 will achieve the same exposure as 1/60th sec at f/8.

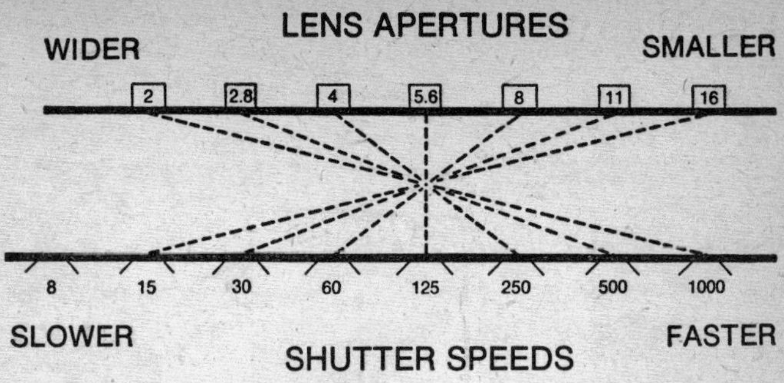

The same applies when less light is available, so that if 1/30th sec at f/2.8 gives a correct exposure, then 1/15th sec at f/4 or 1/60th sec at f/2 could be used too.

Aperture or shutter speed priorities?

A fully automatic camera chooses both aperture and shutter speed for you. But the possibility of pre-selecting shutter speed allows you to freeze moving objects, while aperture choice governs the depth of field and the sharpness zone either side of the point focused on (see diagram). Note that there's always more sharpness behind this point than in front.

This diagram shows the difference between the depth of field at an aperture of f/4 and at f/16. The lens is focused at the point X. The larger area is all in focus at f/16. At f/4 only the smaller area is in focus.

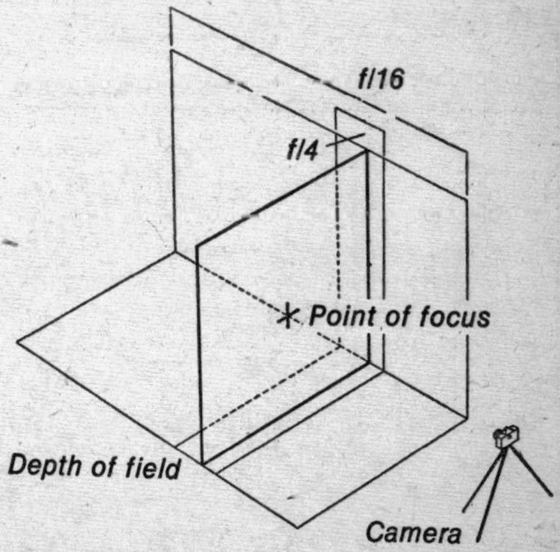

Focusing aids

A lens scale, marked in feet and metres, or self-explanatory picture symbols, are used for non-automatic (or manual) setting. Non-reflex cameras may have a rangefinder, while the focus on an SLR is adjusted until the image appears sharp in the viewfinder. Some of the most up-to-date models focus automatically, when the shutter is pressed.

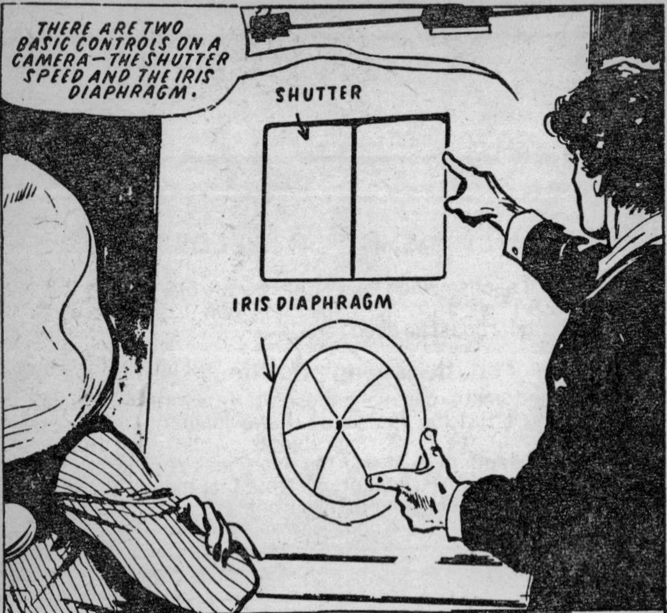
THERE ARE TWO BASIC CONTROLS ON A CAMERA—THE SHUTTER SPEED AND THE IRIS DIAPHRAGM.
SHUTTER
IRIS DIAPHRAGM

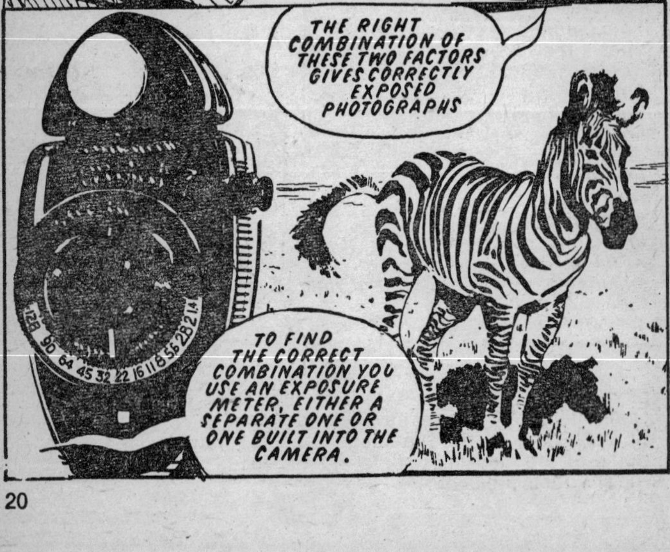
THE RIGHT COMBINATION OF THESE TWO FACTORS GIVES CORRECTLY EXPOSED PHOTOGRAPHS
TO FIND THE CORRECT COMBINATION YOU USE AN EXPOSURE METER, EITHER A SEPARATE ONE OR ONE BUILT INTO THE CAMERA.
128 90 64 45 32 22 16 11 8 5.6 2.8 2 1.4

Measuring light

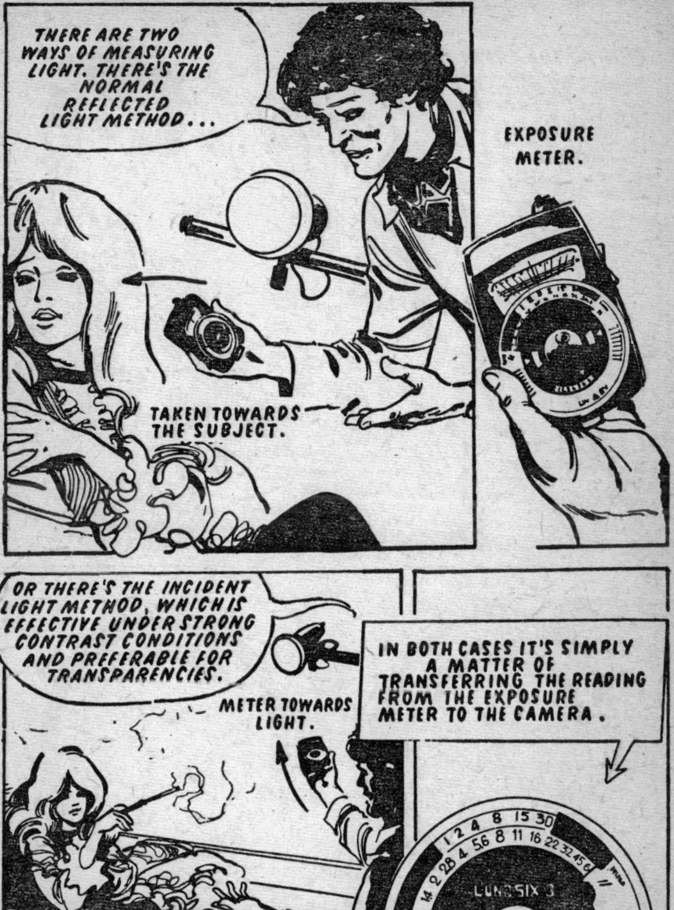

What is an aperture?

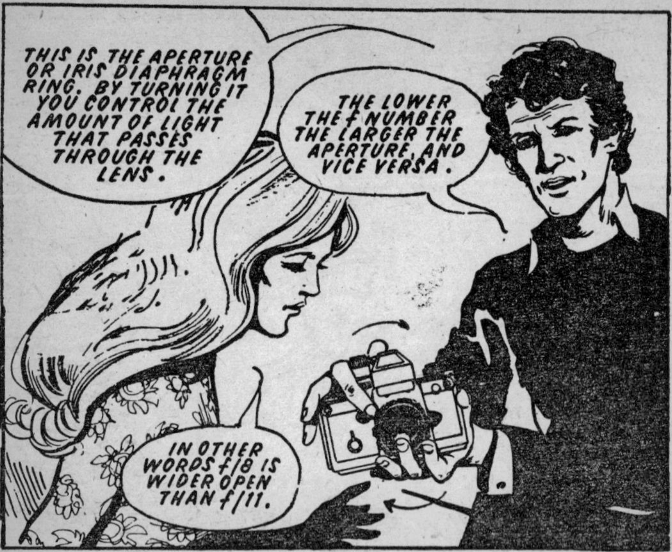

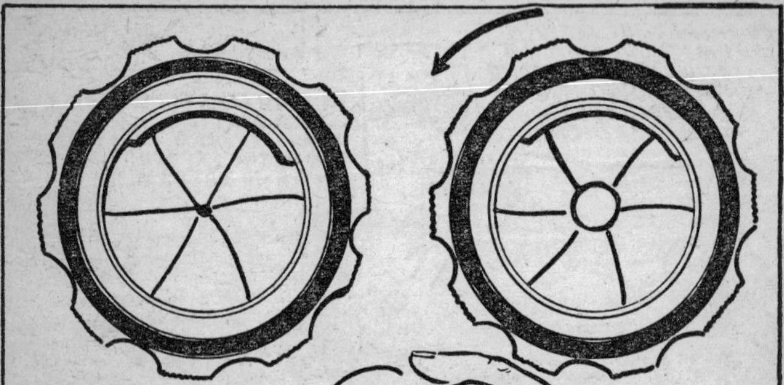

Shutter speeds

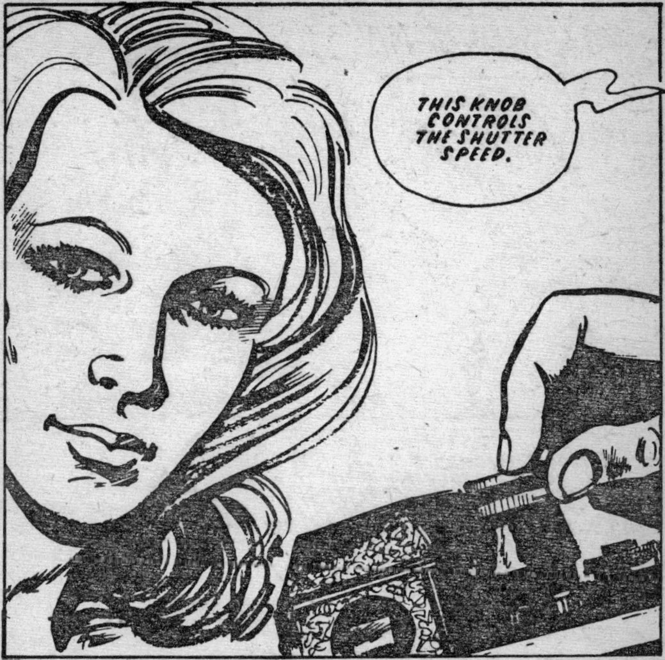

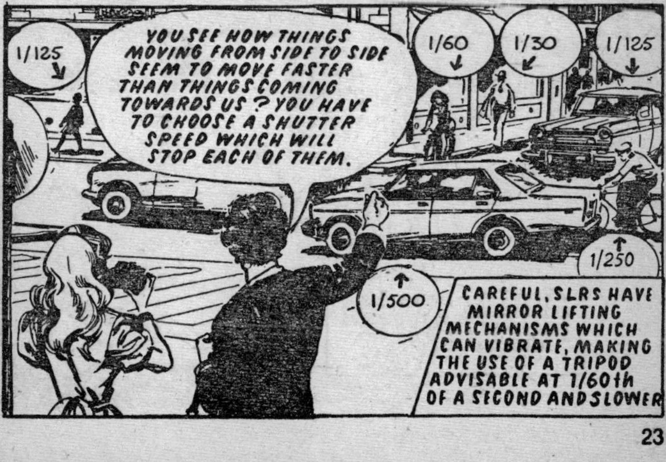

What is depth of field?

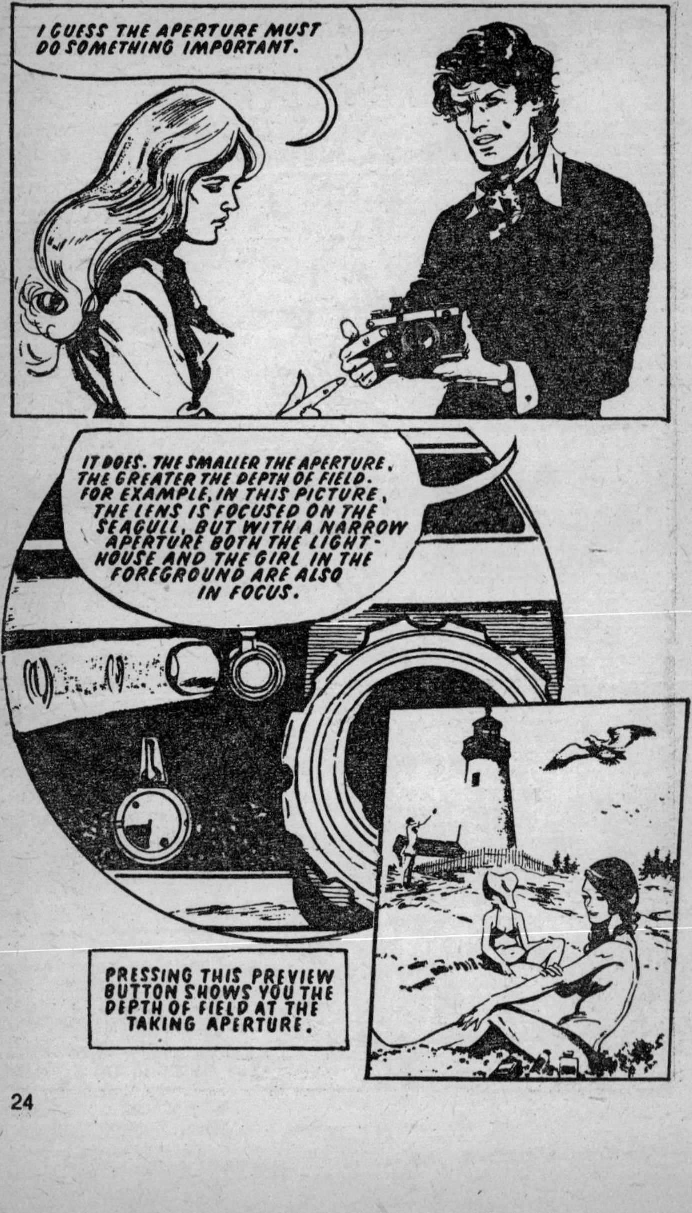

Fix the focus

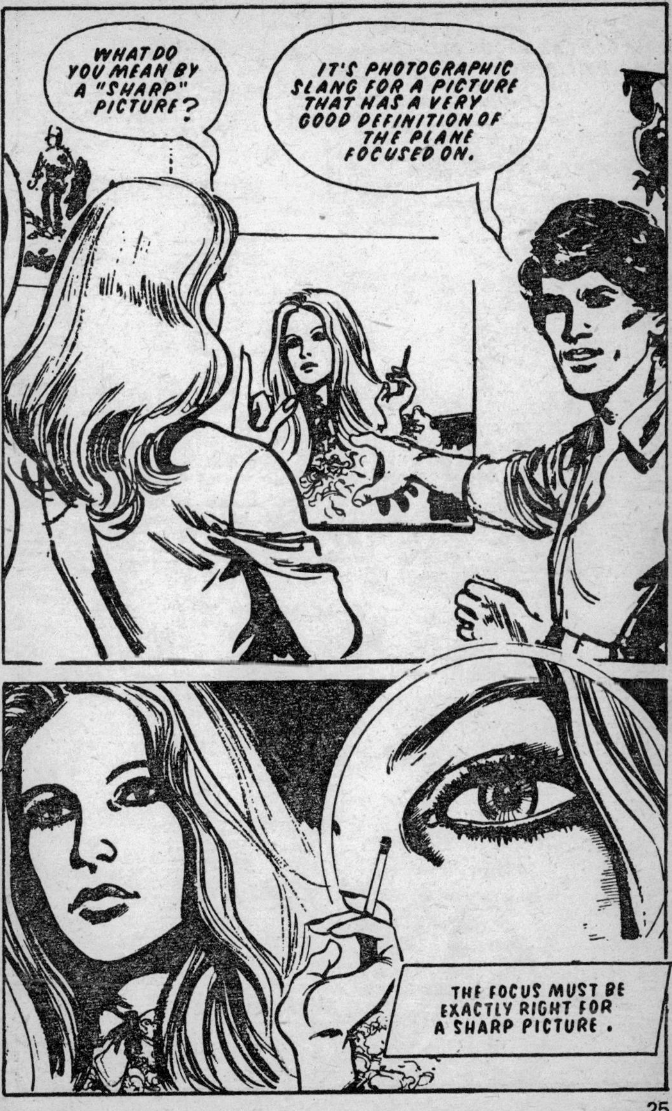

Eye to eye

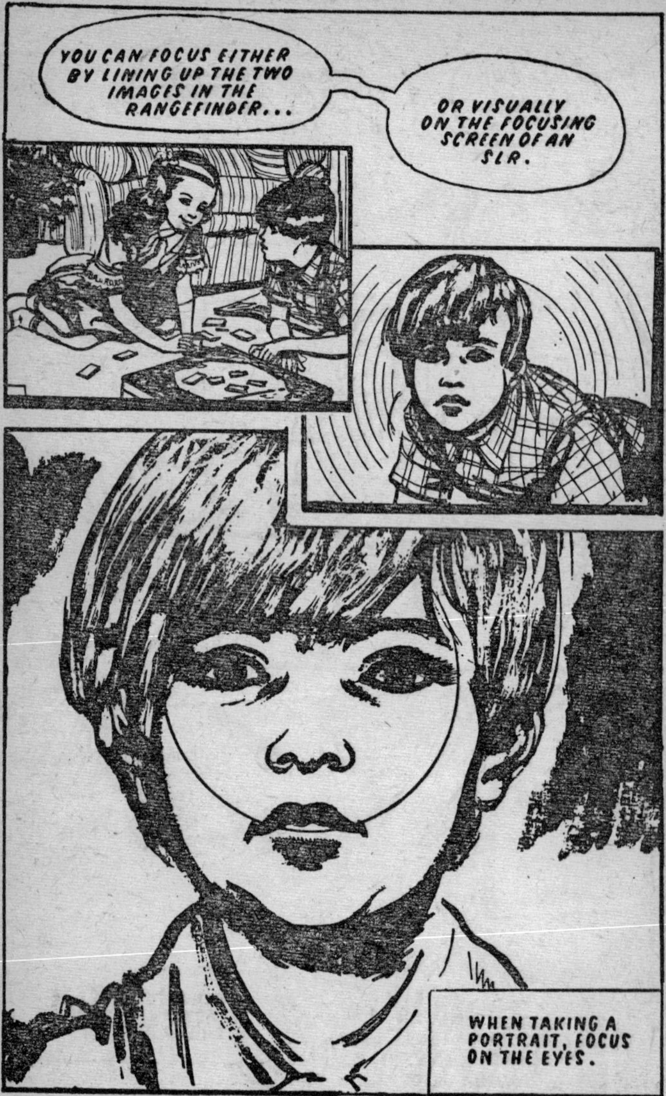

YOU CAN FOCUS EITHER BY LINING UP THE TWO IMAGES IN THE RANGEFINDER...
OR VISUALLY ON THE FOCUSING SCREEN OF AN SLR.
WHEN TAKING A PORTRAIT, FOCUS ON THE EYES.

Vertical or horizontal?

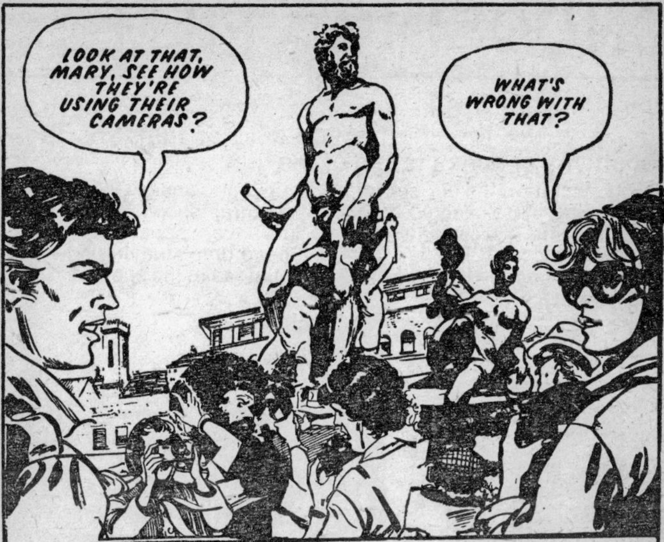

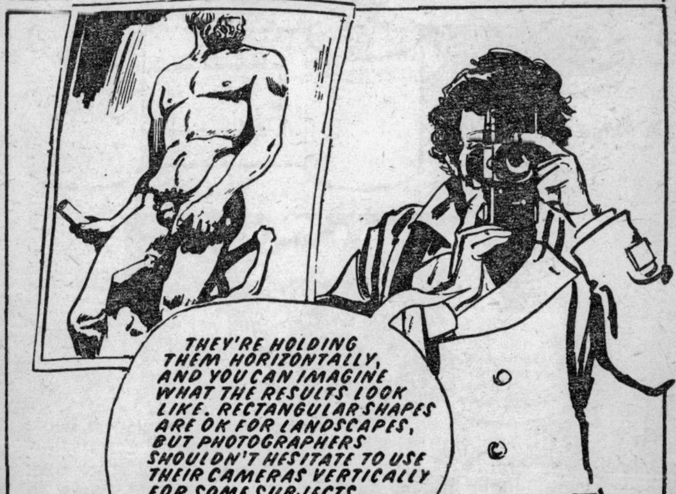

Chapter 4

CHOOSING A FILM

When buying a film, there are three essentials to consider: the format size, the kind of film, and the sensitivity or speed rating of the film.

You must have the correct format to fit your camera. On current models it is most likely to be one of the three shown here. Less common is the 126 cartridge (giving 28cm-square negatives) or the now obsolescent 127 or 620 roll film. Spend time studying how to load and unload the film. Always load or unload in the shade.

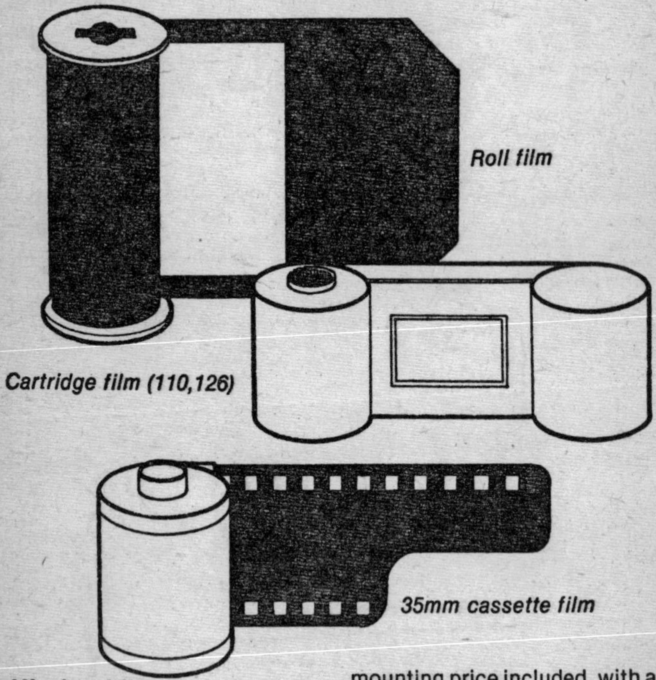

Kinds of film

Colour Transparency

Gives colour slides the same size as the film format. Most have the processing and mounting price included, with a mailing envelope. Others may be processed by the user. There are separate types for use in daylight, with flash or in artificial light.

Colour Negative
Gives negatives from which prints are made, by a film processor or by yourself. Usable in daylight, with flash or artificial light. The colour is adjusted in printing.

Black and white
Gives negatives from which black and white prints are made by enlargement, again professionally or at home.

Instant prints
Give direct prints. Commonest types by Polaroid or Kodak, develops in minutes. A fixed print size and only one print per shot, unless copied.

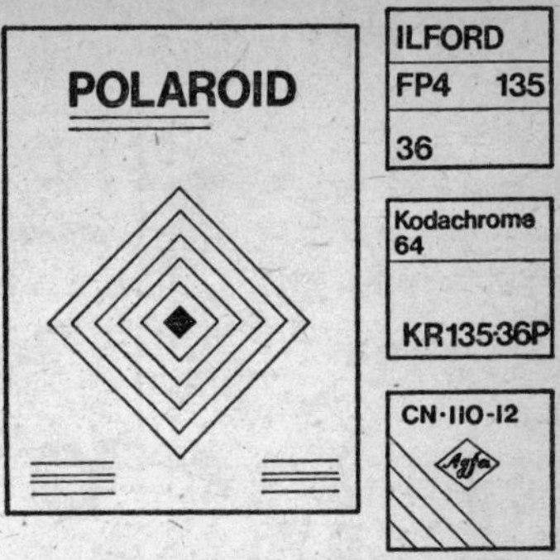

Above: Instant Print film box. Top right: Black and white film box. Centre right: Colour slide film box. Bottom right: Colour print film box.

Special types
Infra-red (for unusual colour effects), copying, duplicating.

Film speed rating

There are two standard measurements called ASA and DIN. Both values are marked on the film box. Here is a list of ratings equivalents in the two measurements.

ASA speeds	**25**	32	40	**50**	64	80	**100**	125	160	**200**	250	320	**400**
DIN speeds	**15**	16	17	**18**	19	20	**21**	22	23	**24**	25	26	**27**

As soon as you have loaded a film, you must set the film speed rating on the camera's film speed dial. Cartridge types are self-setting.

Which speed?

Slower films are fine if there is plenty of light. Fast films are easier to use in poorer light, as they allow for a faster shutter speed or a smaller aperture for more depth of field. Here is an example of the exposures possible with two different films under given lighting conditions.

25 ASA: f/4 + 1/30th sec. or f/2 + 1/125th sec.
200 ASA: f/4 + 1/125th sec. or f/11 + 1/15th sec.

But fast does not always mean best. Slower films give better quality pictures with sharper images and, usually, better colour reproduction. As a rule, use a film of the slowest speed practical for likely light conditions and subject matter.

Slow (25-50 ASA)	For fine detail or static subjects, especially if big enlargements are required.
Medium (64-160 ASA)	Versatile all-round films for most subjects, especially portraits and landscapes.
Fast (200-400 ASA)	For sport and action. For natural light indoors and poor light outdoors.

How film works

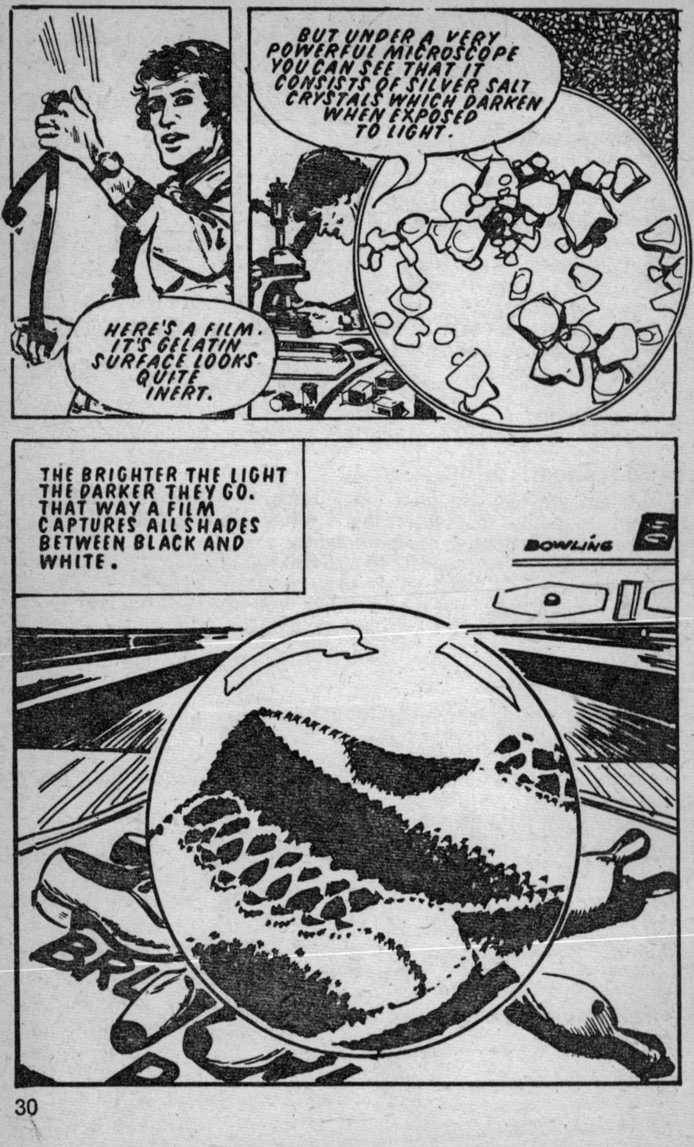

Negatives into prints

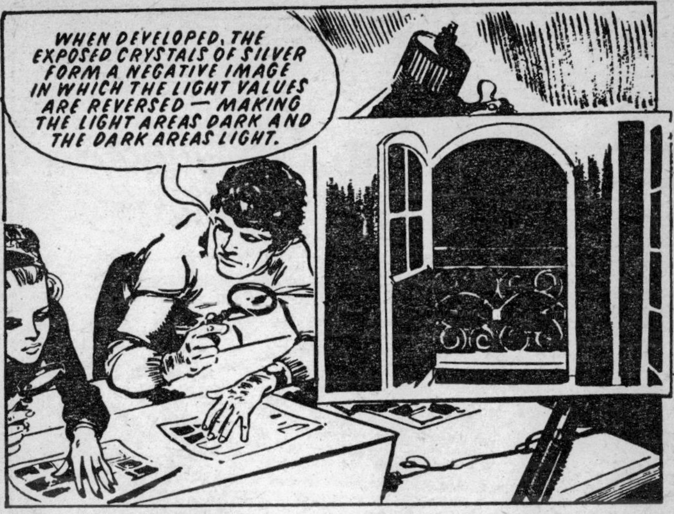

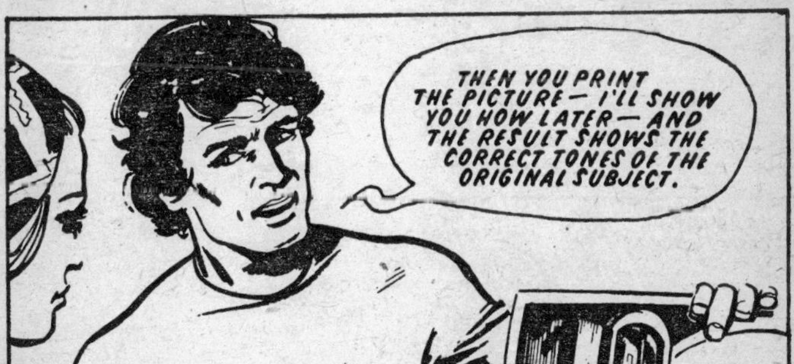

Be positive about slides

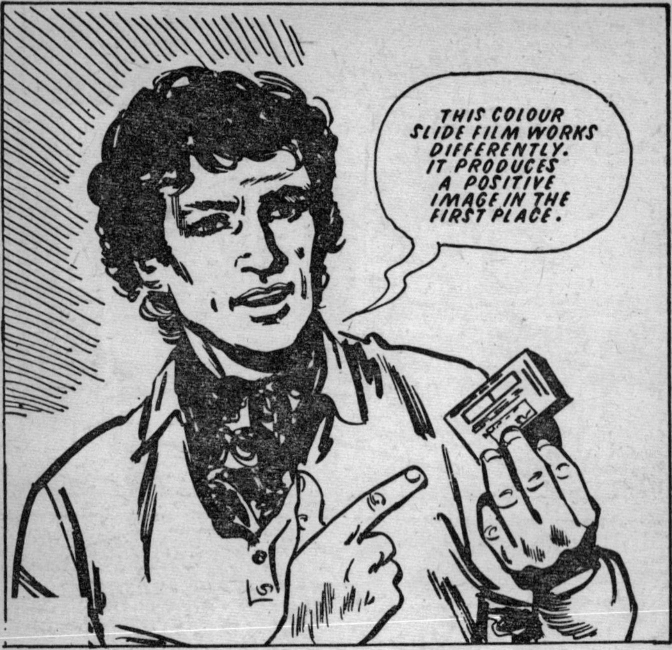

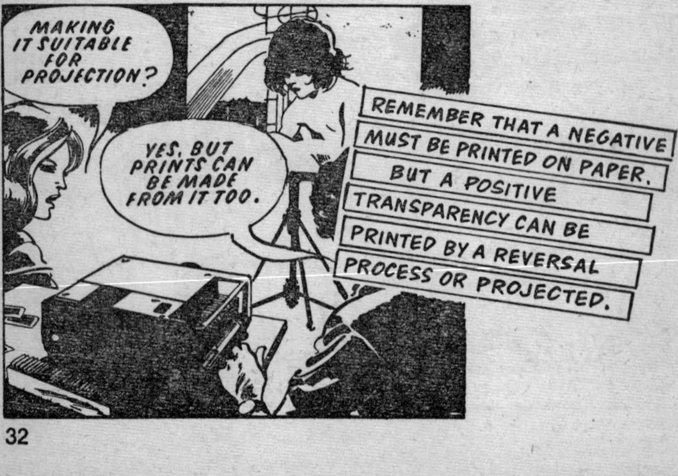

Daylight and artificial light

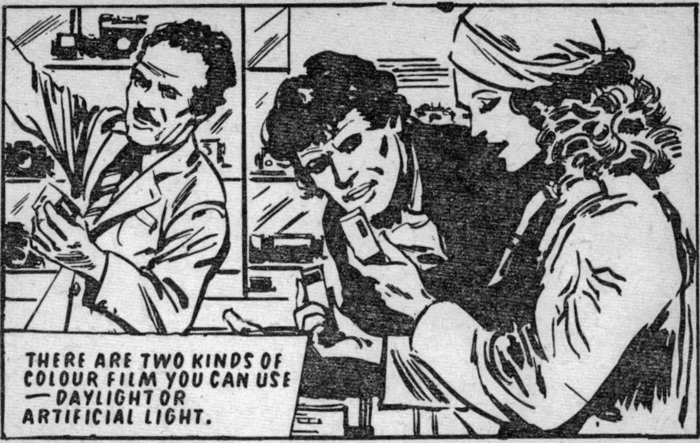

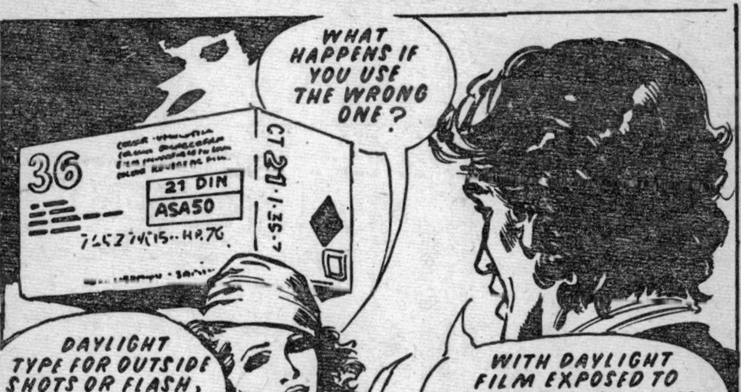

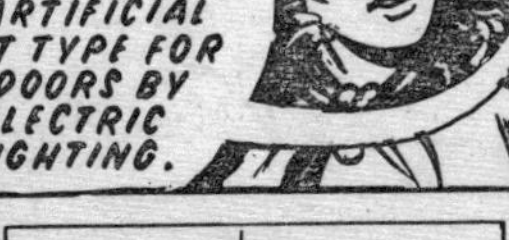

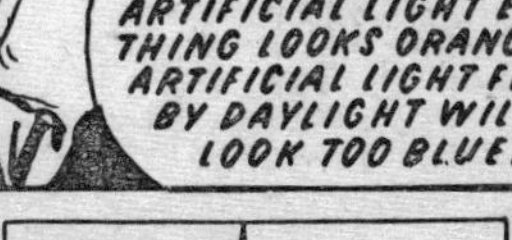

Under and over exposure

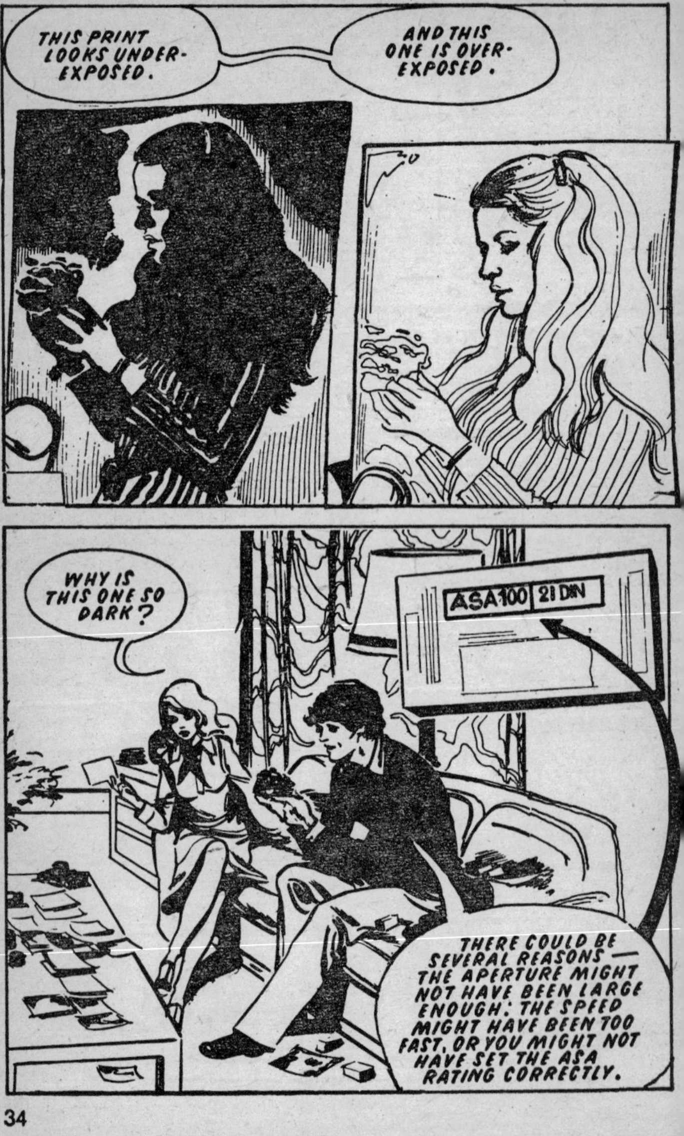

Chapter 5

ALL KINDS OF LENSES

A lens is described in terms of its focal length which affects the angle of view it takes in, and its maximum aperture or opening, which governs its light gathering power. In brighter lighting the lens is stopped down by progressively closing the aperture. It is confusing, but unfortunately established that the measurement of apertures (in f-numbers) uses high numbers (f/16) for small openings and low numbers (f/2.8) for large apertures.

Many cameras have only one lens which cannot be changed. In a 35mm compact, the focal length will be about 40mm, giving about 65° angle of view. The versatile SLR allows the use of a wide range of lenses, with a 50mm lens usually fitted as a standard lens.

The lens on a compact camera will probably have an f/2.8 maximum aperture, which is a moderately fast lens, allowing it to work with relatively little light. Cartridge cameras usually have slower lenses, maximum f/5.6 or even as small as f/11, only permitting shooting in good light, or with a flash.

Focal length and lens coverage

Lenses with focal lengths shorter than the standard 50mm are called wide-angles. The diagram shows the commonest wide-angle lenses for a 35mm SLR.

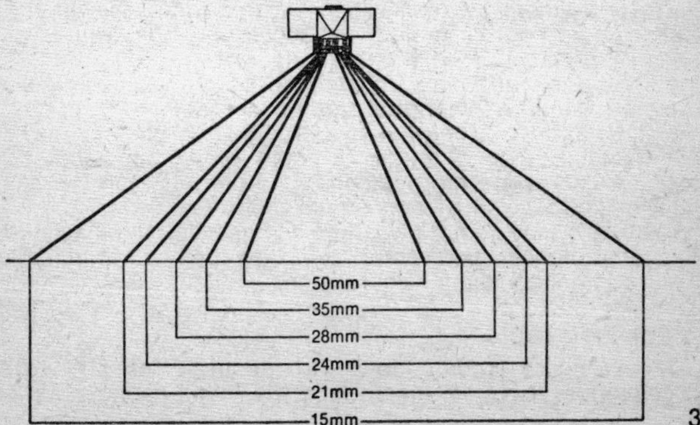

Wider lenses are very useful in cramped conditions. They are also used to give an impression of spaciousness, and sometimes to exaggerate perspective for effect. Very wide lenses, around 15mm, are called fisheye lenses. They cover an angle of 110° or more.

Telephoto lenses

Lenses with a focal length greater than about 85mm are called telephotos. Subjects photographed through them seem much closer so they are good for photographing people unawares and for getting a good full-scale image when taking portraits. The longer telephotos — from 200mm upwards — are used for sports, press photographs taken at a distance and wildlife. The very longest are used for jobs like covering cricket close-up and shots of celebrities from a considerable distance.

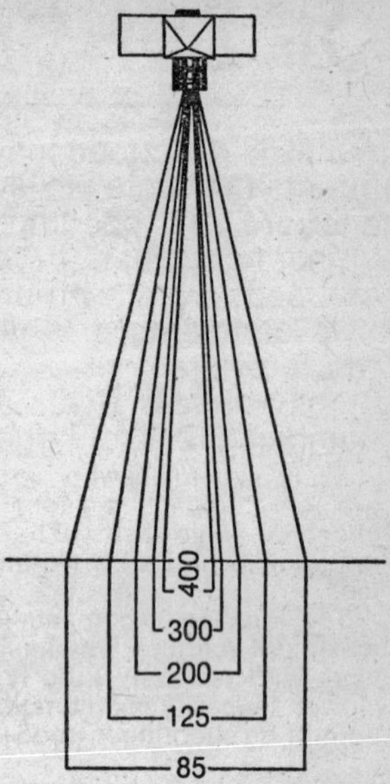

This diagram shows the commonest sizes of telephoto lens used on 35mm cameras, and their fields of view.

Zoom lenses

You will have seen the effects of a zoom lens in television shots, where the camera moves in continuously for a close-up or back for a wider view of the scene. With a zoom lens fitted on an SLR camera you can adjust the focus until the picture viewed seems correctly framed, then take the shot.

Zooms are in effect a number of lenses in one, covering several ranges. Medium telephotos zooms are commonest, covering usually 70mm to 210mm; a wide angle zoom might cover a 24-48mm range; a long telephoto zoom would be, perhaps, 200-500mm. Zooms are more expensive, more bulky on the camera, heavier, and have smaller maximum apertures.

Generally they do not give quite as fine a definition as separate one-length lenses. But versatility makes them worth considering as an addition to your lens collection.

Macro lenses

Most lenses focus down to about 0.6m (2ft) without accessories. A typical macro lens will focus as close as 24mm

(10ins.) A number of zoom lenses also focus very close — they're called macro-zooms. A true macro lens should give an image on the film the same size as the object photographed *eg.* a coin 25mm across should fill the viewfinder. Macro lenses are designed to give their sharpest results at focus point very close to the lens, not at infinity, like normal lenses.

Converters

These are a kind of substitute lens, which extends the use of another. They fit between a camera body and the proper lens and double (with a 2x converter) or treble (with a 3x converter), its effective focal length. With a 2x converter plus a 135mm lens you have a 270mm lens. **Two drawbacks**: unless of very good quality, they diminish the main lens standard, and cut off some of the light. So for a given light value the lens has to be opened up one or two more stops. Converters work better in conjunction with telephoto lenses than standard lenses or wide angles.

Close-up devices

The macro lens is one way of allowing you to take sharp pictures of very small objects. Many other accessories can be fitted in front of, or behind a normal lens to allow you to get closer to your subject.

Close-up lenses are cheap and very easy to use for a moderately close-up approach. They are a kind of spectacle lens that screws to the front of the camera lens, and usually come in three lengths: +1, +2 or +3. The normal focusing range of the lens is used with a close-up lens in place. Unlike other close-up devices, they can be used on non-reflex cameras, though the effect cannot be judged through the viewfinder. Focusing distance is worked out by using a special scale.

Extension rings are sets of rings in different thicknesses which are fitted between the camera body and lens, the magnifying effect being proportional to the thickness of ring used. You need to give more exposure than normal, depending on the extension used. With a 50mm extension on a 50mm camera lens, a film image the same size as the object photographed is given, but an increased exposure of one stop is needed.

Bellows are a much longer and more flexible form of extension, permitting still greater magnification. They give high quality results, especially used with macro lenses and other special close-up accessories, but they are expensive and difficult to use without practice.

Technique

The closer you are, the less the depth of field, so you must use smaller apertures, like f/11 or f/16. You really need a **tripod** too, to hold the camera steady at the necessary slower exposures and to maintain the correct distance from the subject. Extra light eases the problems, so flash is often used for close-ups.

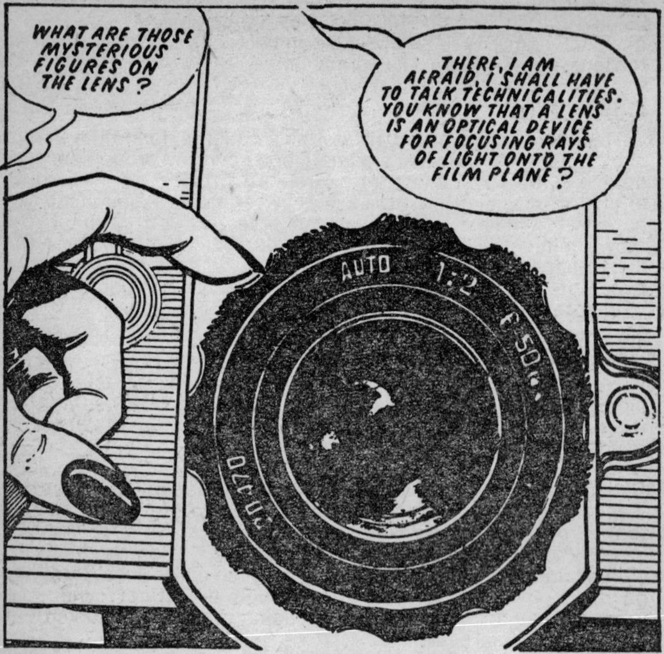
WHAT ARE THOSE MYSTERIOUS FIGURES ON THE LENS?
THERE, I AM AFRAID, I SHALL HAVE TO TALK TECHNICALITIES. YOU KNOW THAT A LENS IS AN OPTICAL DEVICE FOR FOCUSING RAYS OF LIGHT ONTO THE FILM PLANE?
AUTO 1:2 f 50

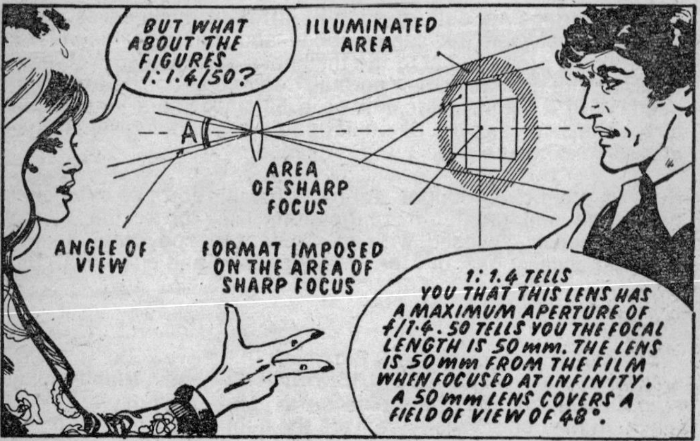
BUT WHAT ABOUT THE FIGURES 1: 1.4/50?
ILLUMINATED AREA
A
AREA OF SHARP FOCUS
ANGLE OF VIEW
FORMAT IMPOSED ON THE AREA OF SHARP FOCUS
1: 1.4 TELLS YOU THAT THIS LENS HAS A MAXIMUM APERTURE OF f/1·4. 50 TELLS YOU THE FOCAL LENGTH IS 50 mm. THE LENS IS 50 mm FROM THE FILM WHEN FOCUSED AT INFINITY. A 50 mm LENS COVERS A FIELD OF VIEW OF 48°.

Wide angle lenses

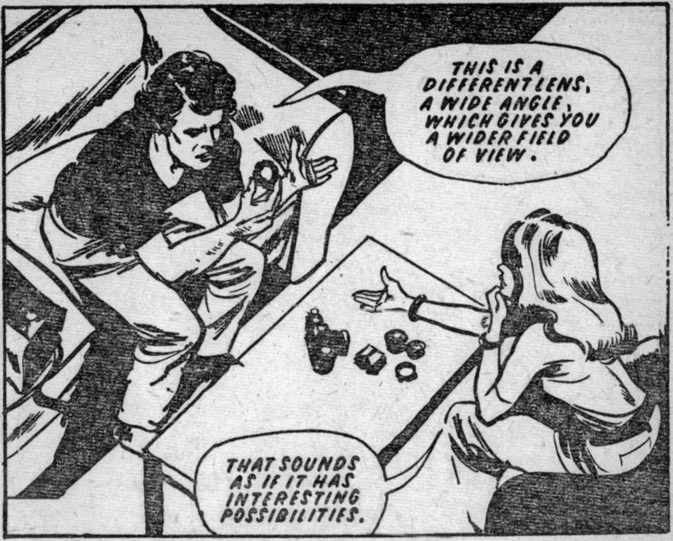

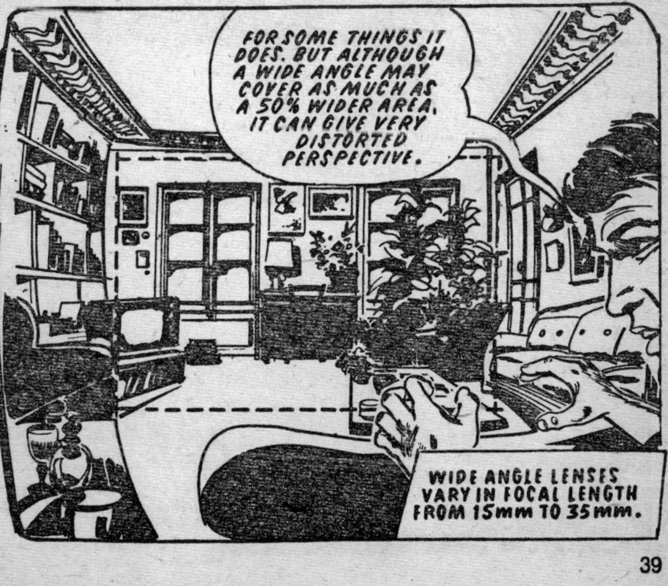

Telephoto lenses

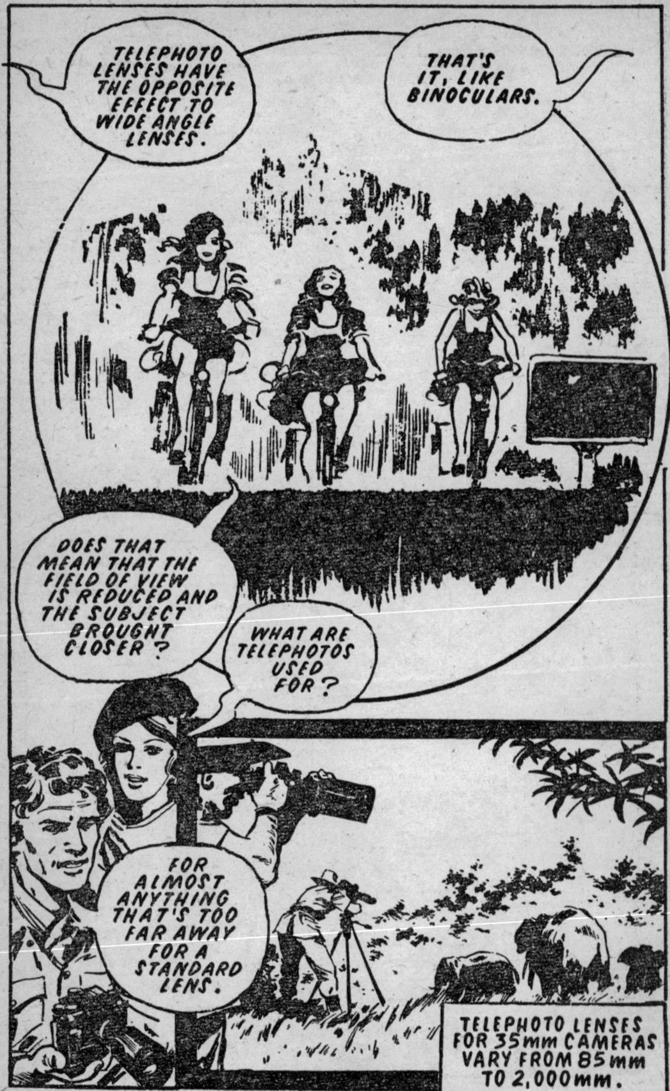

Zoom lenses

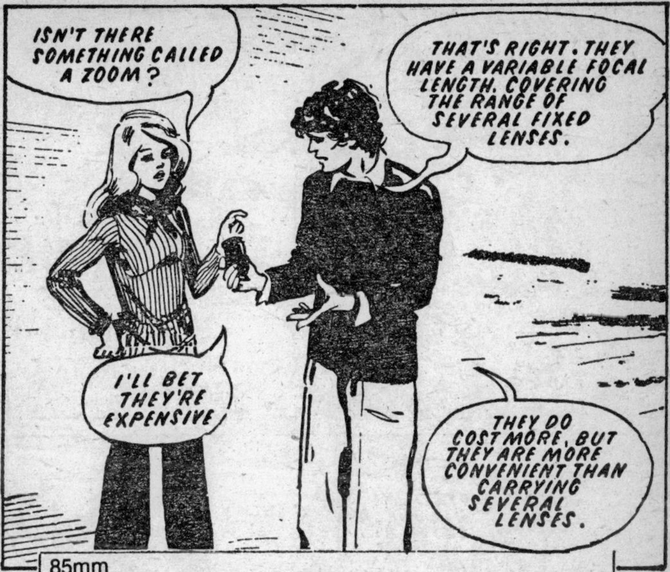

ISN'T THERE SOMETHING CALLED A ZOOM?
THAT'S RIGHT. THEY HAVE A VARIABLE FOCAL LENGTH, COVERING THE RANGE OF SEVERAL FIXED LENSES.
I'LL BET THEY'RE EXPENSIVE
THEY DO COST MORE, BUT THEY ARE MORE CONVENIENT THAN CARRYING SEVERAL LENSES.

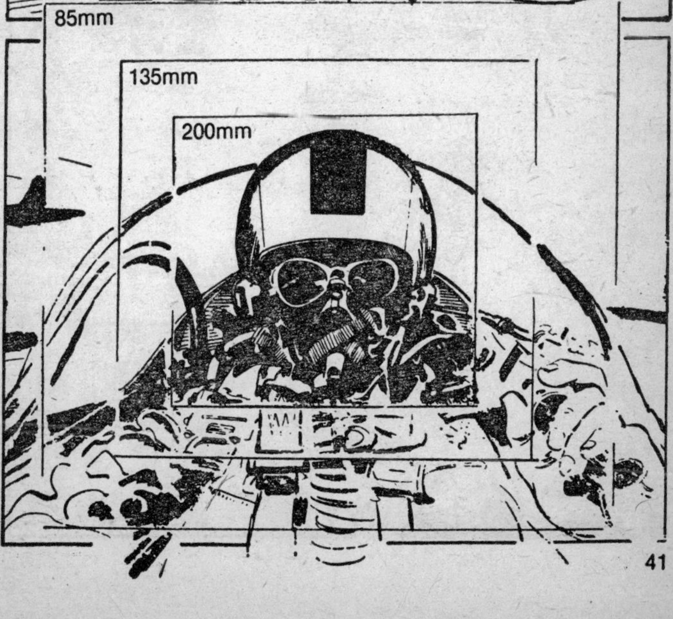

85mm
135mm
200mm

Macro lenses

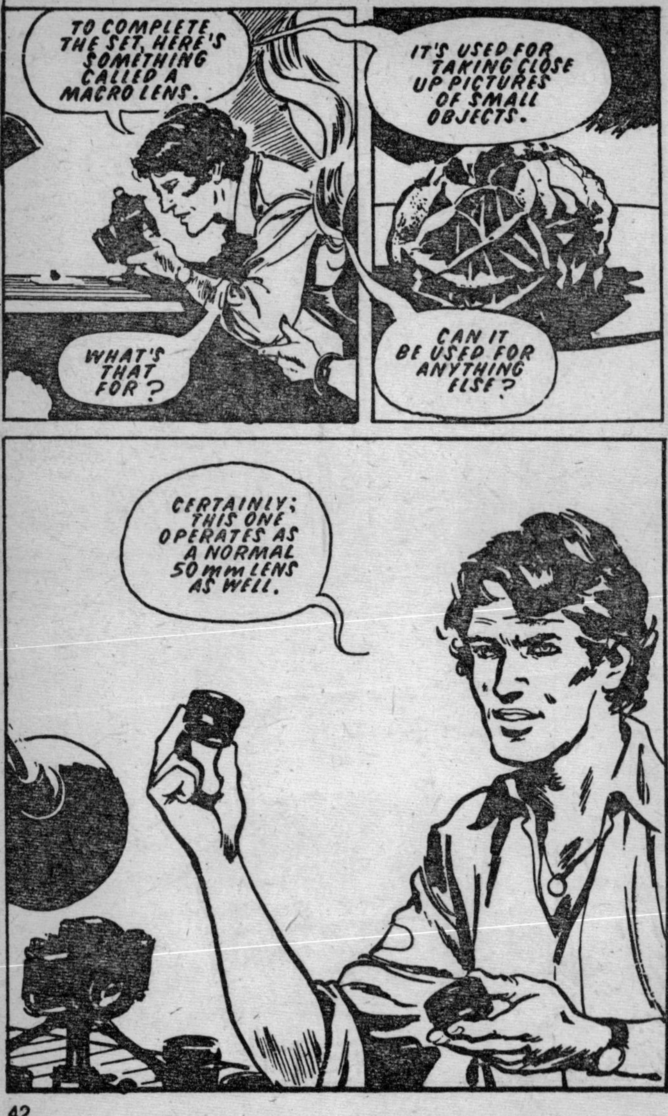

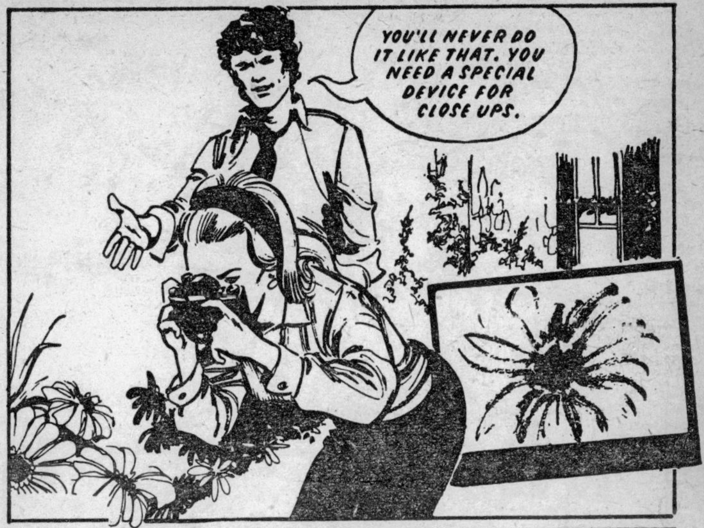
YOU'LL NEVER DO IT LIKE THAT. YOU NEED A SPECIAL DEVICE FOR CLOSE UPS.

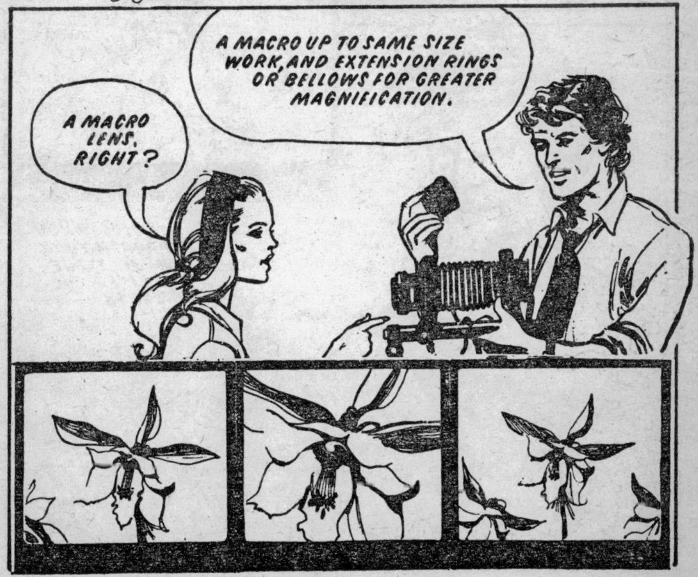
A MACRO LENS. RIGHT?
A MACRO UP TO SAME SIZE WORK, AND EXTENSION RINGS OR BELLOWS FOR GREATER MAGNIFICATION.

Beware the breeze

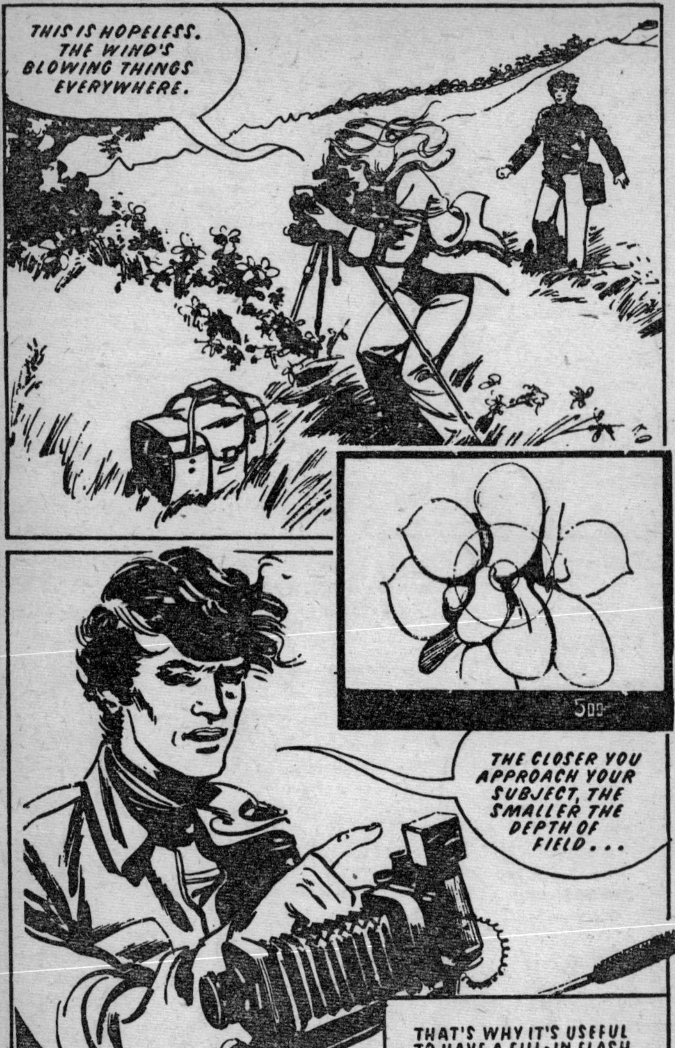

Chapter 6

COPING FROM THE START

Many people do not make proper use of their cameras. They simply hold the camera, look through the viewfinder and press the shutter release. Simple isn't it? And much easier than coping with settings and choosing lenses! But in fact millions of photos are spoiled, because the photographer does not cope with the camera confidently nor study the viewfinder image intelligently.

Hold the camera correctly

Camera shake is the great enemy. Hold the camera rock steady and press the release very smoothly. Practice makes perfect, so practice early on without film in the camera to avoid wasting shots later. Don't hold too fiercely, or your hands will shake.

At speeds below about 1/60th sec. you will need to hold extra steadily to avoid camera shake. Remember, at even higher speeds with a telephoto lens, the effects are magnified. Use something to steady the camera and yourself, or use a tripod at the slowest speeds.

Study the viewfinder

If your pictures aren't good enough, you aren't close enough! In most beginners' pictures you'll need to look hard to make out just what is supposed to be the main point of the picture. Figures appear with acres of meaningless space around them. People are often shown full figure, when head and shoulders would be more effective; close crop the picture by cutting out anything that does not add to the picture's message.

Be wary of too close a viewpoint and distortion. If you fill the frame with a full face portrait, using a wide-angle lens, you have to move in very close, causing distortion, such as noses appearing much too big. A medium telephoto lens avoids this and allows you to work at a more comfortable distance.

Leaning verticals

Another common fault is crooked verticals and horizontals. Take care to ensure that the horizon is absolutely level and make sure that lines of vertical features, like buildings, are parallel to the side of the viewfinder. This is especially important when holding the camera vertically.

Problems arise when you tilt the camera up to include the top of a building, as the sides converge. Stand further back and at a higher level, or emphasise the tilt for a deliberately dramatic effect.

Natural lighting

In the early stages you are more concerned about having enough light to give a correct exposure. If there is not enough, you might think that using a flashgun is the complete answer. Not necessarily.

In many cases the lighting already available, daylight (even indoors) or room lighting, is sufficient. With fast colour or black and white films and modern lenses used at full aperture, you can take pictures in quite low light levels. The pictures look much more natural, as daylight gives a softness that is hard to imitate using artificial lights, especially flash, which is sometimes harsh and unpredictable. Many photographers are afraid to use their lens at a full open aperture of, say f/2, because there is so little depth of field, but that itself is often a bonus as the subject will be shown sharply etched against a soft, out-of-focus background.

Flash for convenience

Flash is often necessary indoors for action-packed activities like parties. Modern electronic flashguns take care of the technical problems that bother novices. You can buy flashguns to match many cameras which automatically set the correct synchronisation speed. It's usually 1/60th sec. but see your camera instruction booklet.

With simpler manual flashguns, setting the right aperture for correct exposure is decided by consulting a calculator dial or table on the flashgun.

Modern computer-type guns make flash exposure much easier. You just set one aperture for a given film rating. The gun then automatically, within a specified but wide range, regulates the amount of light emitted according to the distance from the subject. A sensor on the gun measures light reflected back from the subject, from this the flash assesses the distance and cuts short the light when the exposure is adequate.

Hold right, not tight

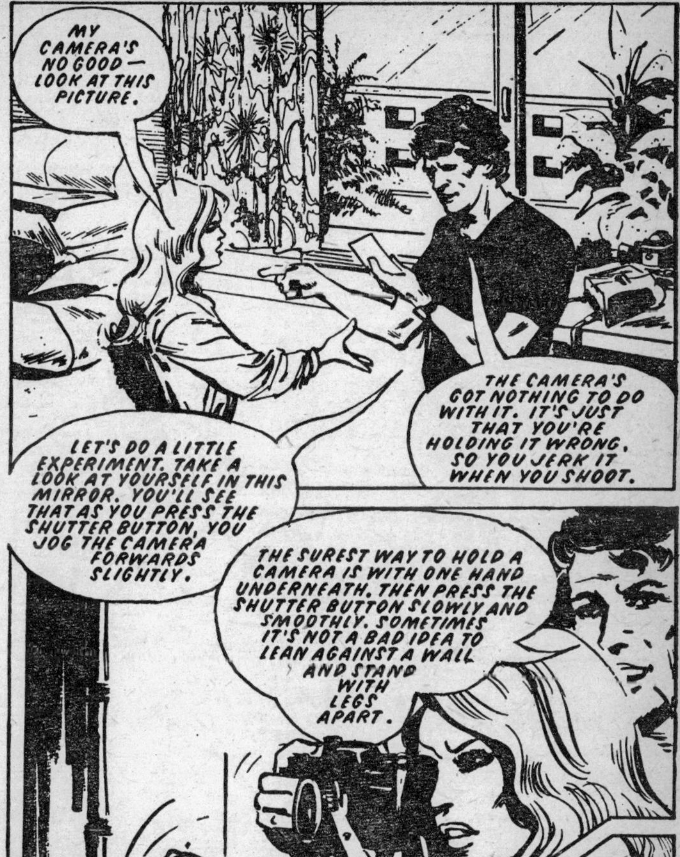

Which lens?

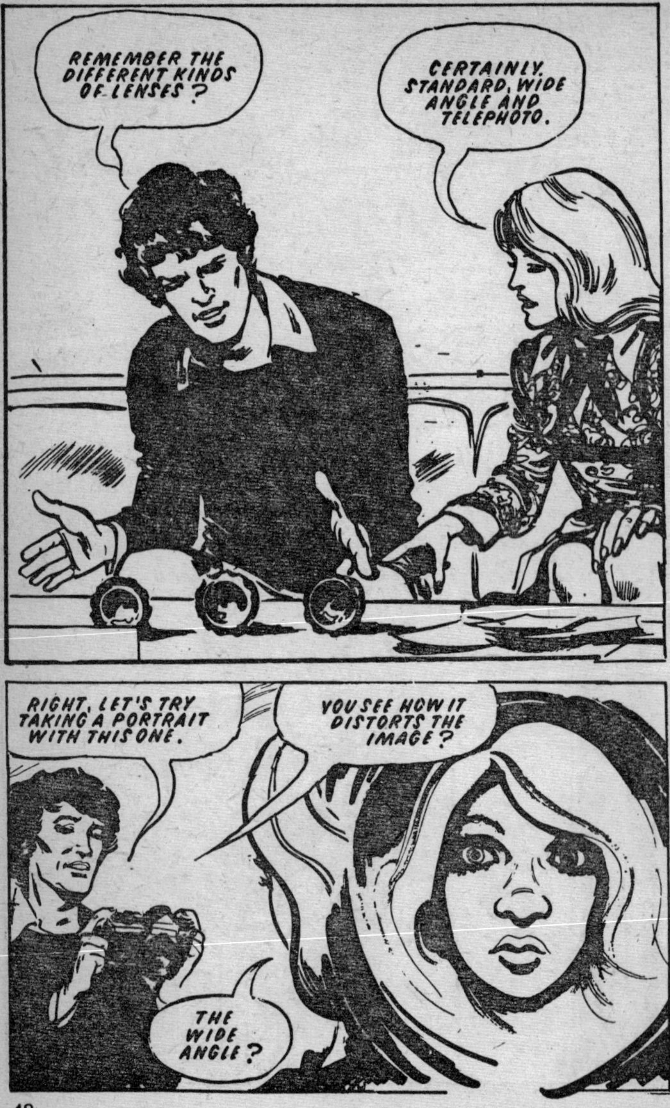
REMEMBER THE DIFFERENT KINDS OF LENSES?
CERTAINLY. STANDARD, WIDE ANGLE AND TELEPHOTO.
RIGHT, LET'S TRY TAKING A PORTRAIT WITH THIS ONE.
THE WIDE ANGLE?
YOU SEE HOW IT DISTORTS THE IMAGE?

A telephoto for portraits

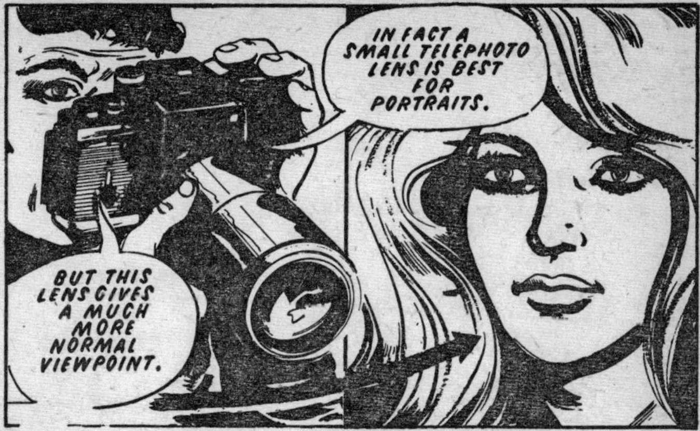

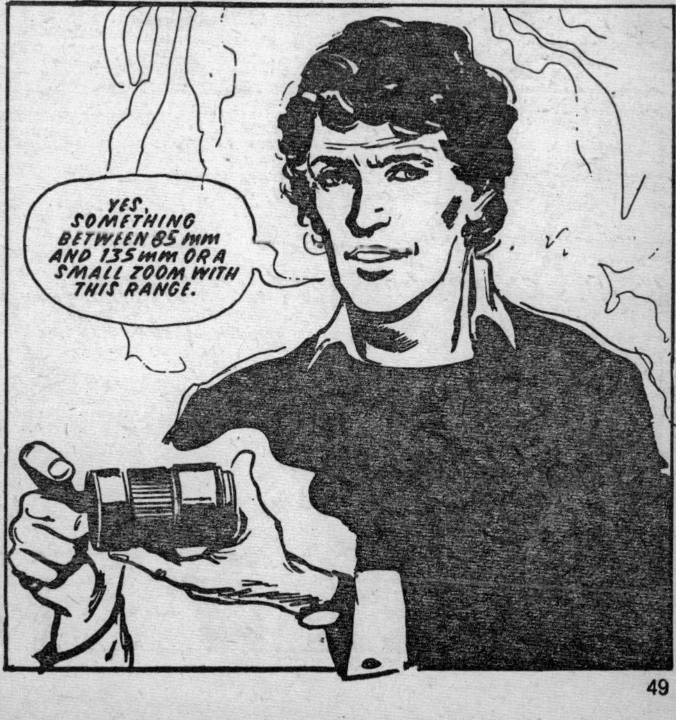

When it's too dark

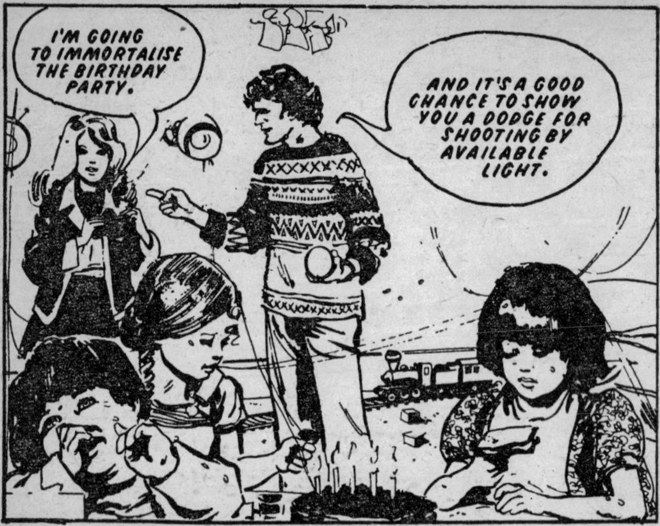

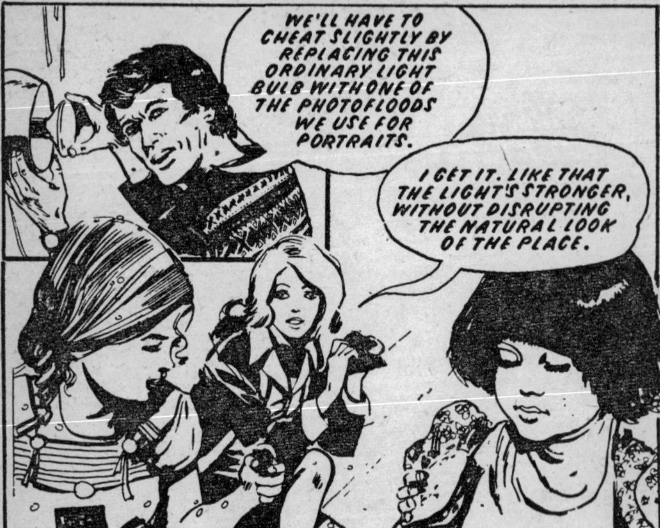

Uprate the film

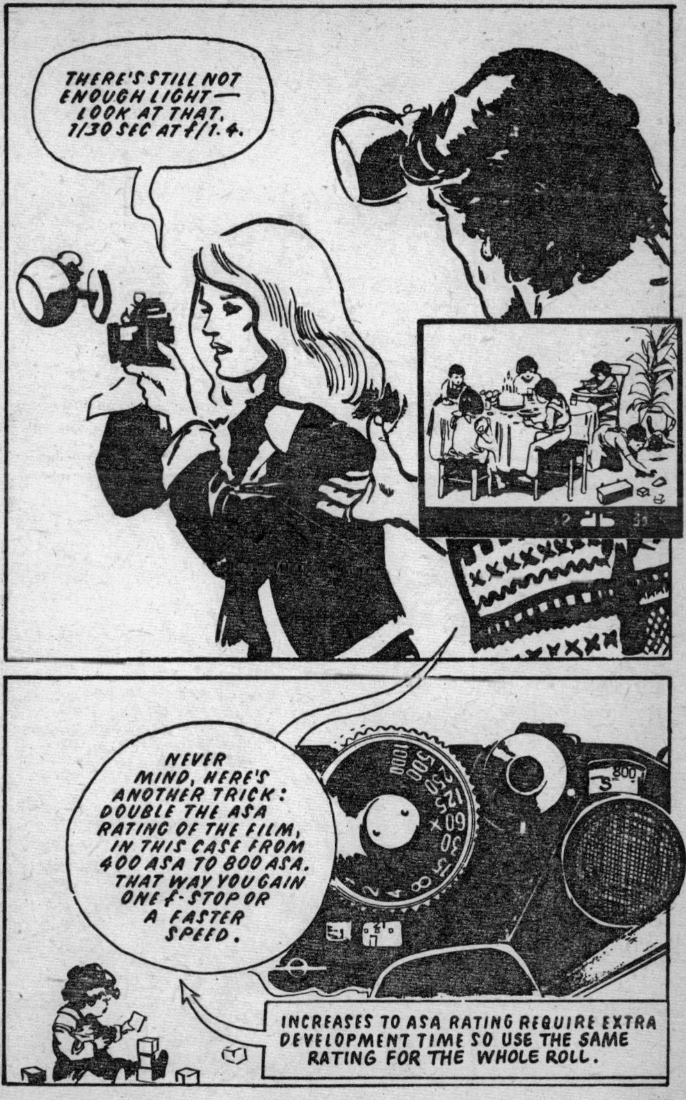

Meter it right

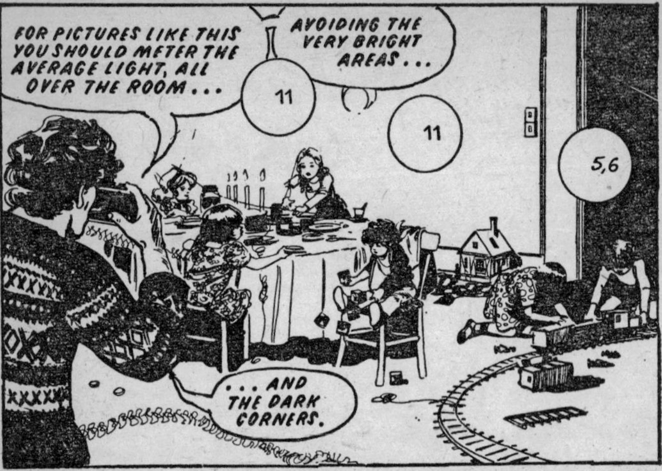

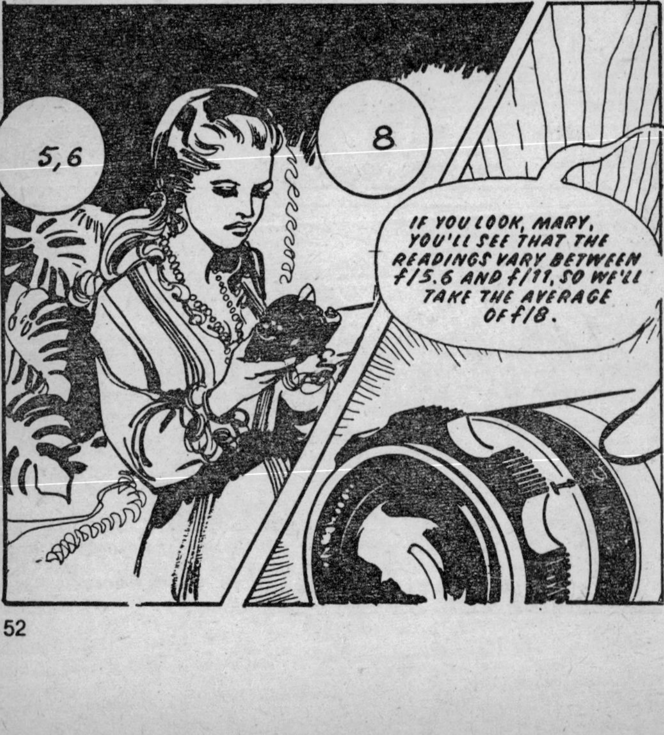

Pocket sunshine

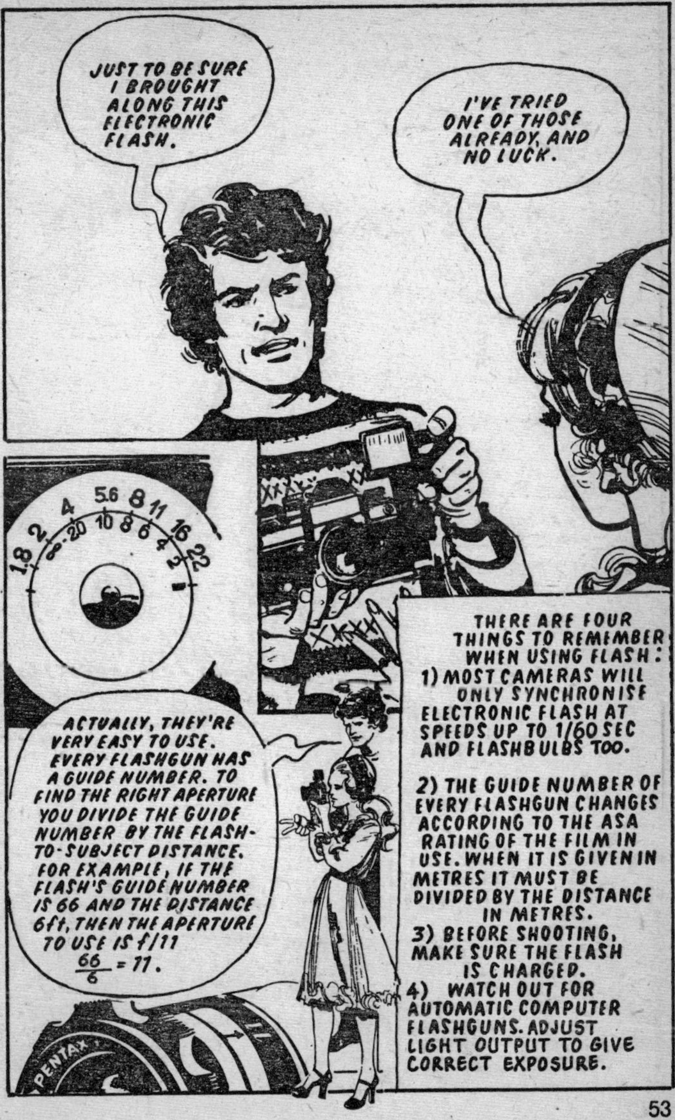

Bounce flash

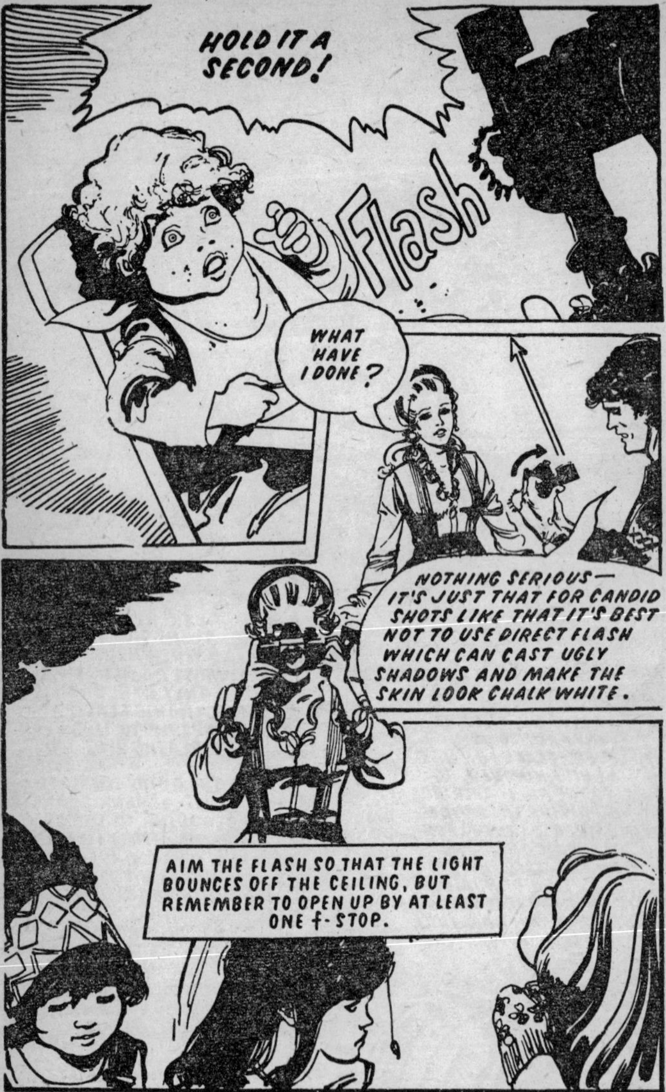

Chapter 7

TAKING PICTURES INDOORS

You can often photograph people indoors without additional lighting by using fast film. Ordinary room lighting may be strong enough for adequate exposure, as might window light. Both give natural-looking results. But if photos show too much light and shade difference (too much contrast), or room lights are not sufficient or well placed, flashguns or special tungsten lights called photofloods can be used.

Nowadays electronic flashguns are so popular, versatile and cheap, that tungsten lighting is rarely used. Tungsten lighting gives a less natural studio atmosphere, creates heat and needs longer exposures. It's worth trying however, if only to study just how proper light positioning can greatly improve a portrait. Using special self-contained mirror photoflood bulbs in conventional light fittings keeps equipment costs low, but beware that the heat from them doesn't damage the fittings.

The classic lighting set-up, as in the diagram, gives flattering modelling, and avoids too much contrast. Position the main light

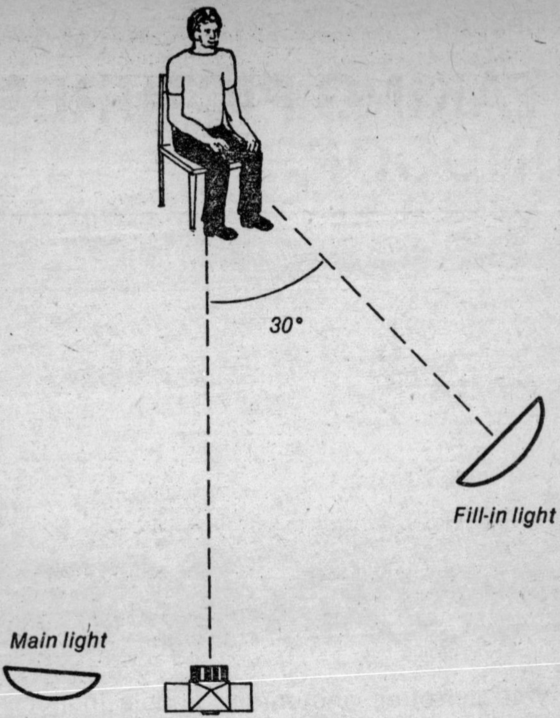

first, at about the angle shown and higher than the sitter. Then switch on the fill-in light which is just to lighten shadows. For more fill-in with colour photos, place it a little nearer than for black and white. Aim for this softer contrast also when photographing children or women. Screens of gauze in front of the lights will help to soften the lighting further.

When you understand the effects of this basic lighting, you can use an additional light perhaps on the background, or a concentrated beam from a small spotlight directed from behind to give lustre to hair, taking care that it does not spoil the effect of the main light.

Using flash well

The only real disadvantage of flash is that you cannot study the way it lights the subject before you use it. For an approximate idea you could hold a lamp in the position of the flash. Generally though, flash used in the photoflood mainlight position, above and to the side, will give a similar effect. The greatest advantage of flash is that it's very short, brilliant light bursts permit short exposures, so freezing movement.

Lightening the shadows is most easily done by having someone hold a white reflecting card near the subject, on the opposite side of the flash. A nearby white wall is most effective, or you can achieve softer, natural overall lighting by using the bounce-flash technique.

Bounce flash

The flash is directed, not at the subject, but at the ceiling or sometimes a wall, and the light thus reflected onto the subject. As the flash is weaker you have to increase the normal flash exposure, on average by two stops.

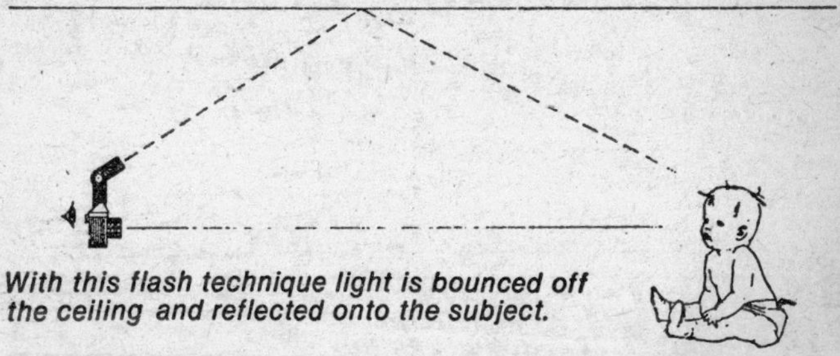

With this flash technique light is bounced off the ceiling and reflected onto the subject.

A computer flash gun usually compensates automatically for the lost light power.

Bounce flash does not work very well in very large rooms; also beware of coloured walls or ceilings, which may come out on colour film. It is very practical for groups like children at parties, as the lighting is more evenly spread over the people nearest to, and farthest from, the camera.

Many flash guns have a head-tilting facility for bounce flash. Some have accessories for widening or concentrating the light beam, for different lenses, and for varying power output.

Thyristor computer guns have a power-saving circuit for battery economy. Many units have accessory fittings to enable them to be used from the mains electricity.

Another point to remember is the recycling time — the time necessary for the unit to be ready for the next flash. This is indicated by a neon ready-light, the average time being around 10 seconds. If you take another shot too soon it may be wasted for lack of light.

Flash gun with a tilting head

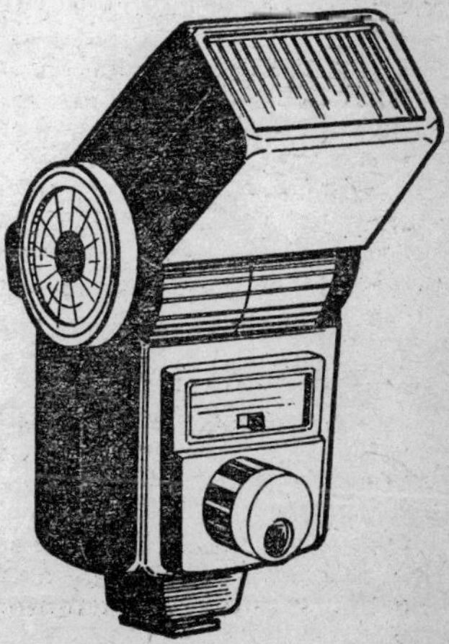

One light is enough

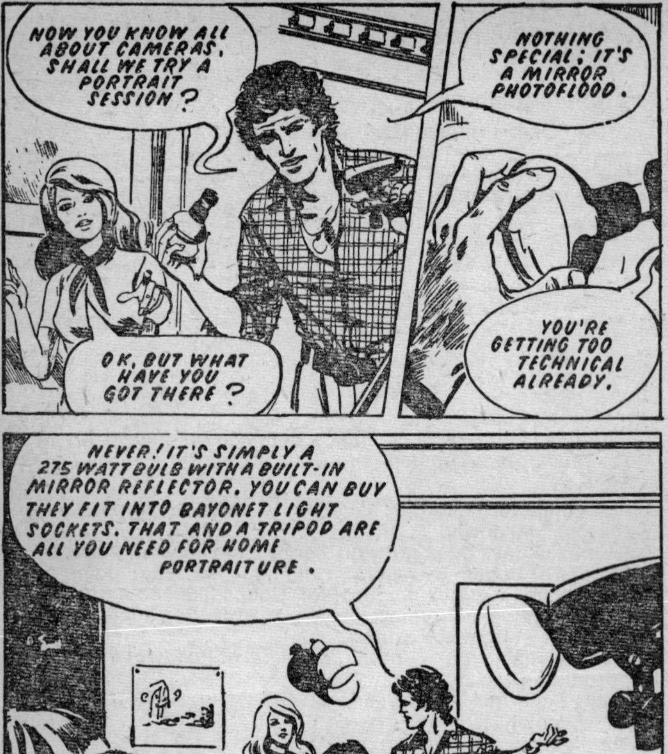

From what distance?

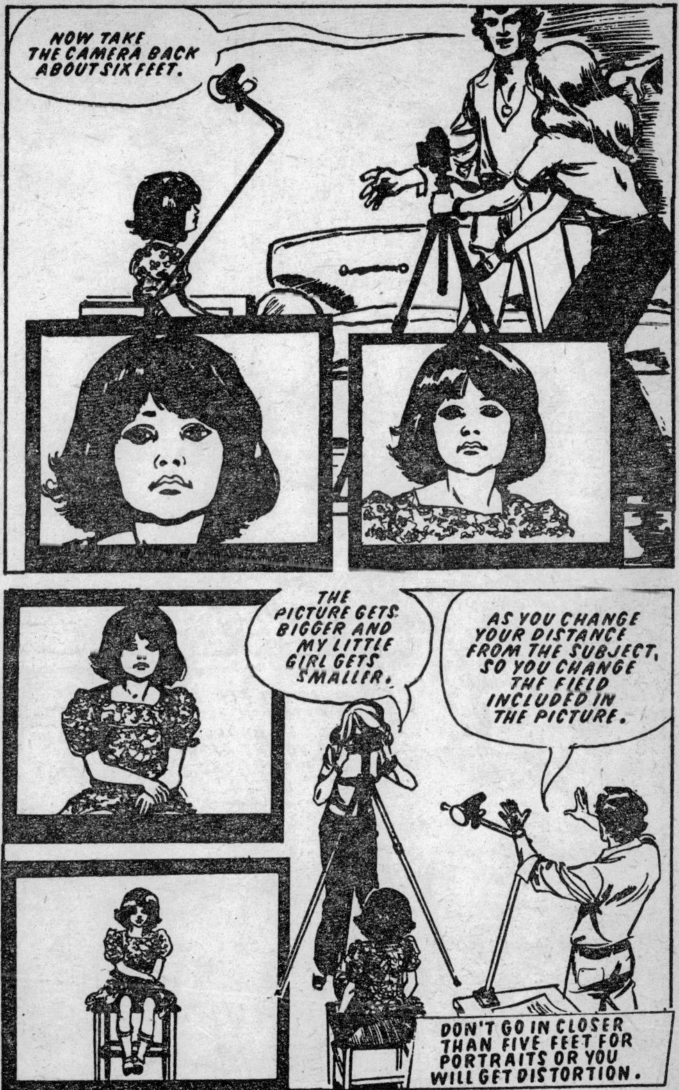

Above and to the side

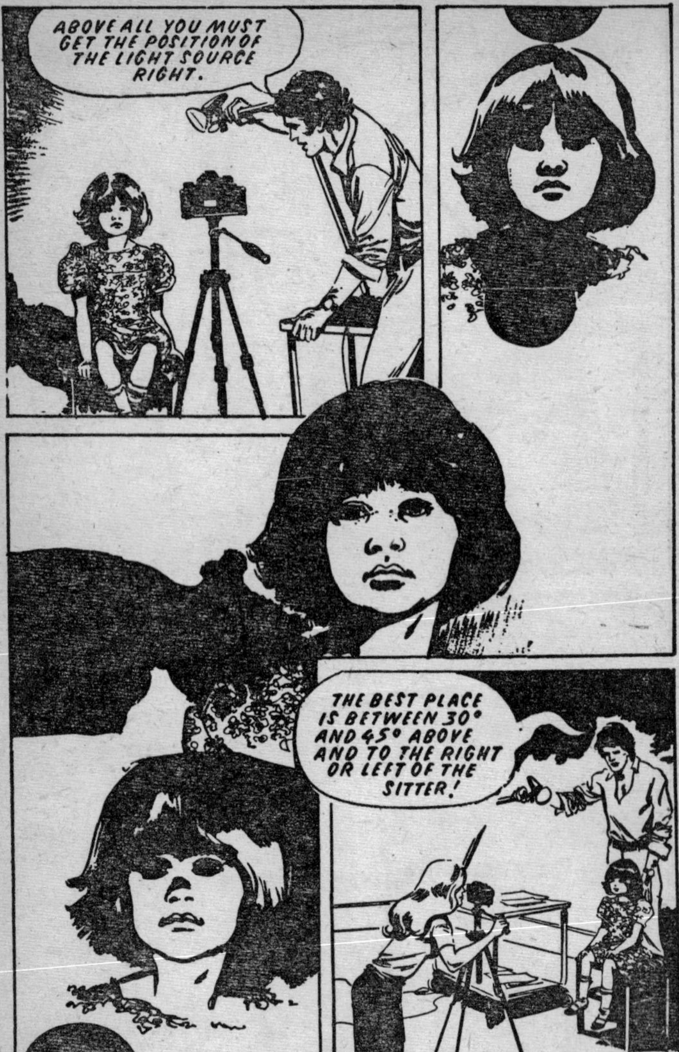

Two lamps at a time

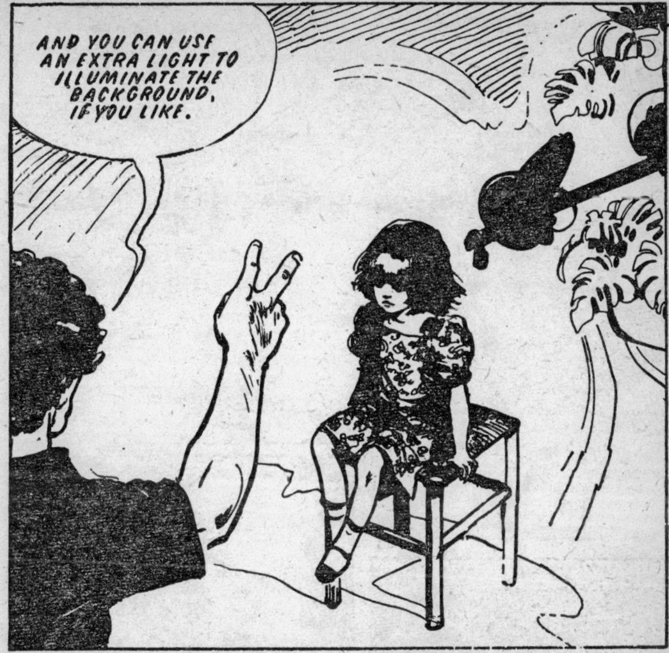

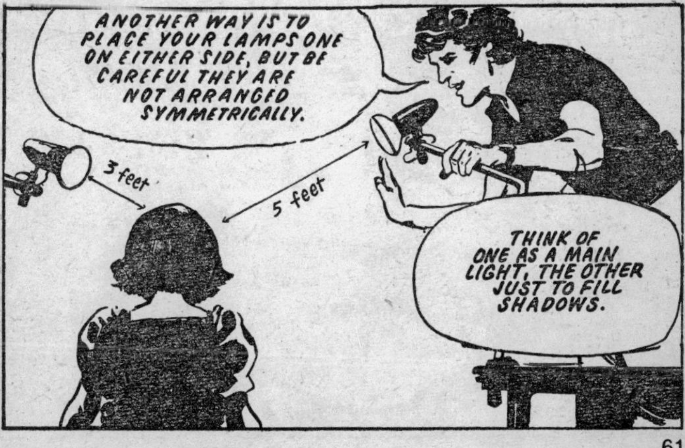

Paper reflectors

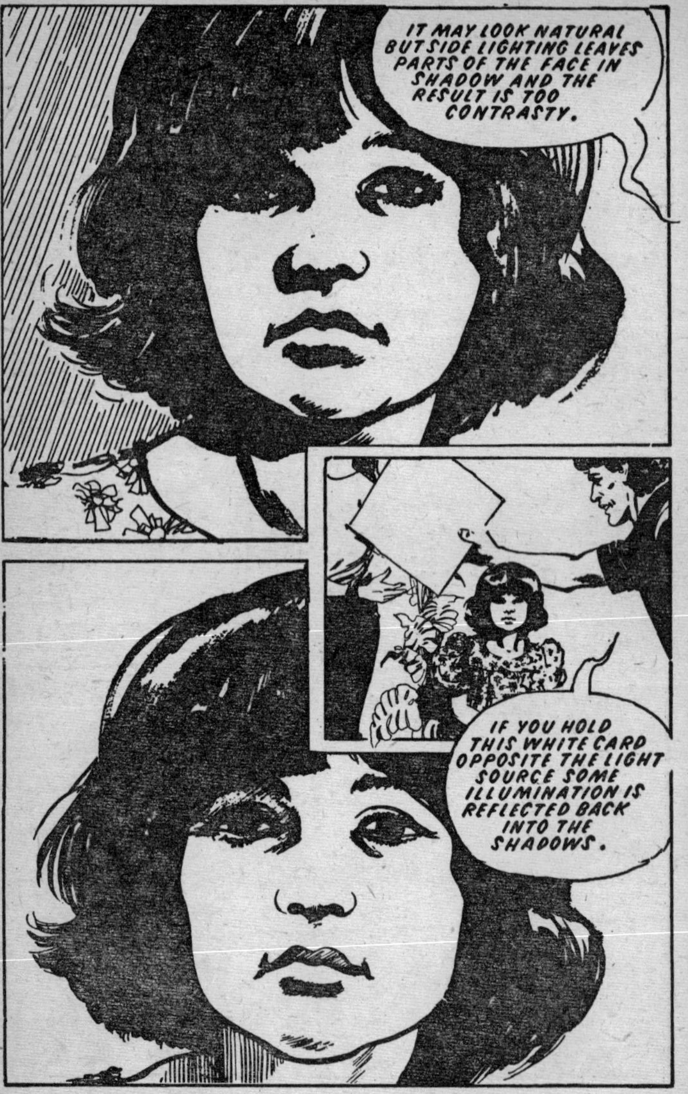

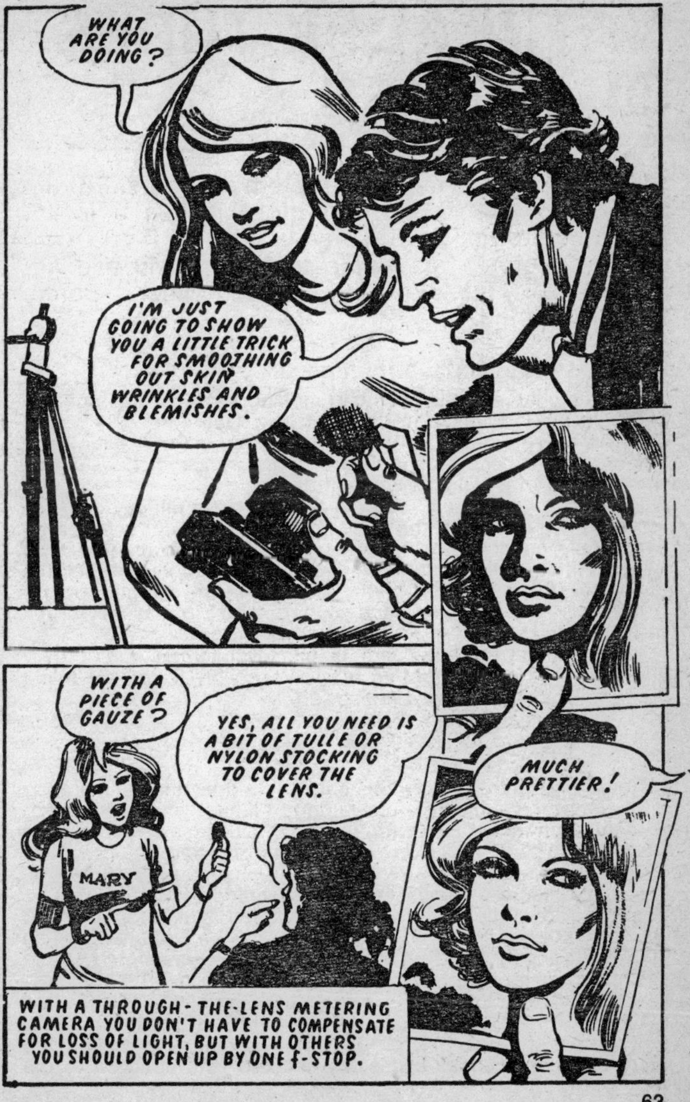
WHAT ARE YOU DOING?
I'M JUST GOING TO SHOW YOU A LITTLE TRICK FOR SMOOTHING OUT SKIN WRINKLES AND BLEMISHES.
WITH A PIECE OF GAUZE?
YES, ALL YOU NEED IS A BIT OF TULLE OR NYLON STOCKING TO COVER THE LENS.
MARY
MUCH PRETTIER!
WITH A THROUGH-THE-LENS METERING CAMERA YOU DON'T HAVE TO COMPENSATE FOR LOSS OF LIGHT, BUT WITH OTHERS YOU SHOULD OPEN UP BY ONE f-STOP.

Chapter 8

NATURAL PICTURES OUTDOORS

Sufficient light is rarely a problem outdoors. But the way you make use of the light makes a lot of difference to the quality of your photos. If you want to take pictures of people that are lively and not spoilt by silly mistakes, there are a number of points to keep in mind.

Avoid strong frontal sunshine

The last chapter explained how much portraits can be improved by using lights or flash in the right way. Outdoors, you cannot manoeuvre your main light source, the sun. But having your subjects in the best place in relation to the sun, and choosing the right time to shoot, makes a great difference.

Countless holiday pictures are taken around midday with the victims lined up facing the sun and camera. Result: screwed up eyes, deep shadows in the eye sockets and flat, uninteresting lighting. Strong, harsh sunlight does *not* give good portraits. It's far better if you can take pictures earlier in the morning or late afternoon. Then you can place your subjects so that they are lit from one side.

It's even better if the sun is partly obscured. Light, hazy sunshine is the best lighting of all, especially if you are using colour film, as the contrast will be soft.

Backlighting for portraits

For really attractive portraits, shoot with the sun behind and to one side of the subject, remembering to adjust your exposure to suit this lighting. A straightforward exposure reading will make the face too dark, so you have to open up the aperture one or two stops, depending on the strength of the sunlight.

Auto-exposure cameras may have a compensation device to make this adjustment. Look in the camera booklet. If not, then set the film rating dial as if for a slower-rated film e.g. change from 100ASA to 25ASA just for the backlit shot. *Do remember* to reset to the correct rating afterwards.

With such backlit portraits, the sun highlights the subject's hair with an attractive halo effect and the face is softly lit. To avoid light reflections from this frontal light inside the lens spoiling the picture, screw a cheap accessory called a lens hood on to the front of the lens.

Fill-in flash

Competent photographers like this way of combatting back-lighting contrast and providing sufficient facial fill-in lighting, because it allows both background and subject to be correctly exposed. With the previous method you have to sacrifice the background slightly as the extra exposure bleaches it out.

The flash is fitted on the camera in the usual way. You measure the exposure and choose a combination which allows a shutter speed to synchronise the flash, usually 1/60th sec., and the appropriate aperture.

The secret is to achieve the right lighting balance, without too much flash added to spoil the natural daylight appearance. *Example:* say the daylight exposure is 1/60th sec. and f/11, and you are 2.5m (8ft) from the subject. If the correct setting at that distance for flash is f/8 (consult the table on your flashgun), then the balance is about right. Aim at one stop difference for fill-in daylight flash. If the flash setting is less, cut down the flash power by covering it with one or more handkerchief or tissue layers. Experiment to find the best balance.

Taking them naturally

Many people think that they don't photograph well, but it is usually the photographer who doesn't! Never say smile and have people grinning fixedly, while you mess about with settings. It's much better to catch them more naturally. Wait until they look up, and quickly take a picture of their alert expression. Take pairs or groups of people in conversation, looking at something together or strolling along, rather than standing like soldiers in a line.

Take children at play; they're bound to be looking lively. Why not picture acquaintances while they're working? Including something of a person's natural surroundings says more about his or her personality.

Avoid awkward angles

Ask someone to stand about 2m (6ft) away holding an arm outstretched towards the camera. That photo will speak volumes about perspective effects.

Using a wide-angle lens for a portrait won't have very welcome effects. Big nose won't like the result! A medium telephoto, about 90mm, is best for portraits while standard lenses are all right for children, as they have smaller features.

Look beyond the subject in the viewfinder for trees or lamposts growing from heads. A slight change of angle makes all the difference.

If the background competes with the subject for interest, shoot from slightly lower, outlining the subject against a plain sky. Use narrow depth of field to your advantage; a wide aperture makes the background completely fuzzy, so the subject shows in sharper relief.

All that free light!

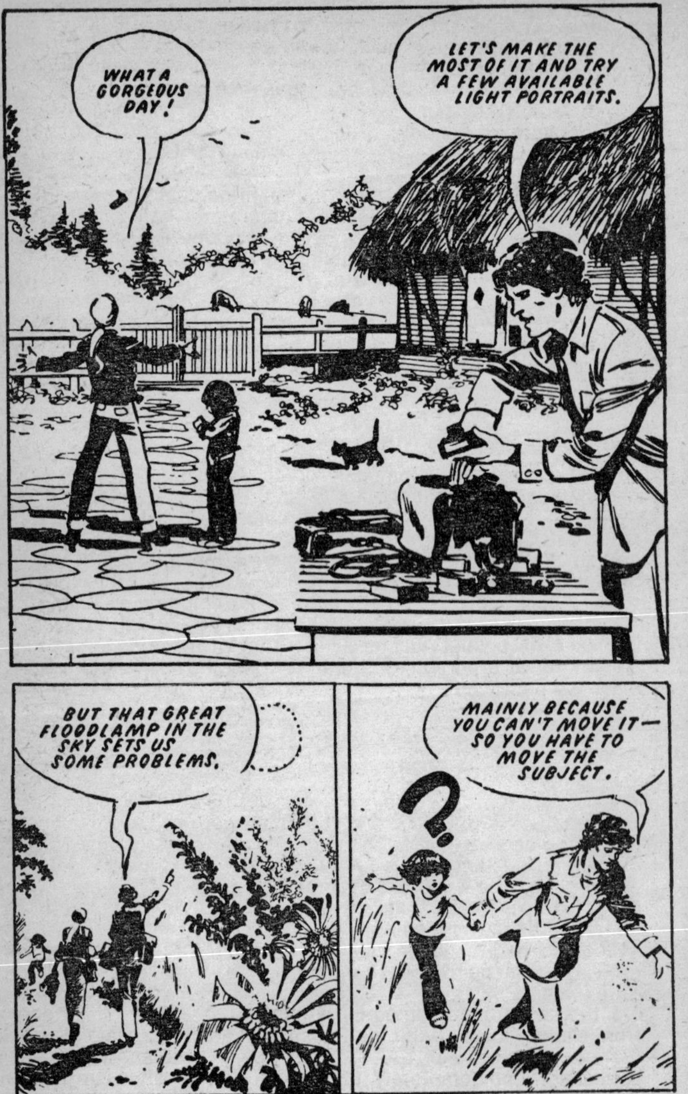

Make the most of sunpower

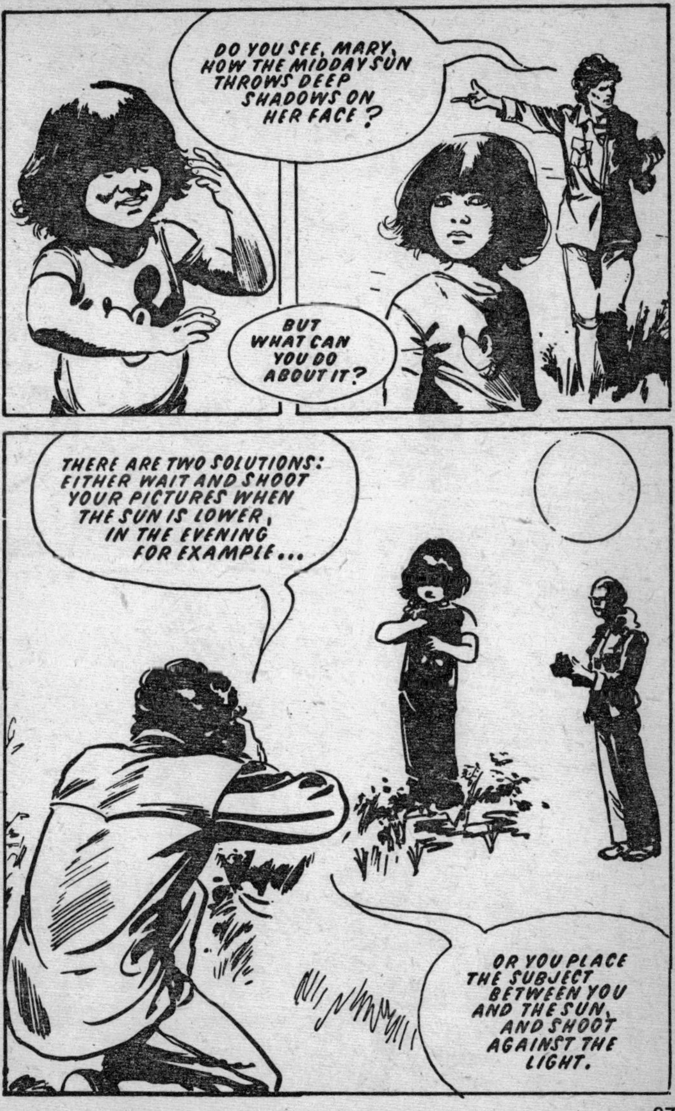

«Back to the sun» is bunk

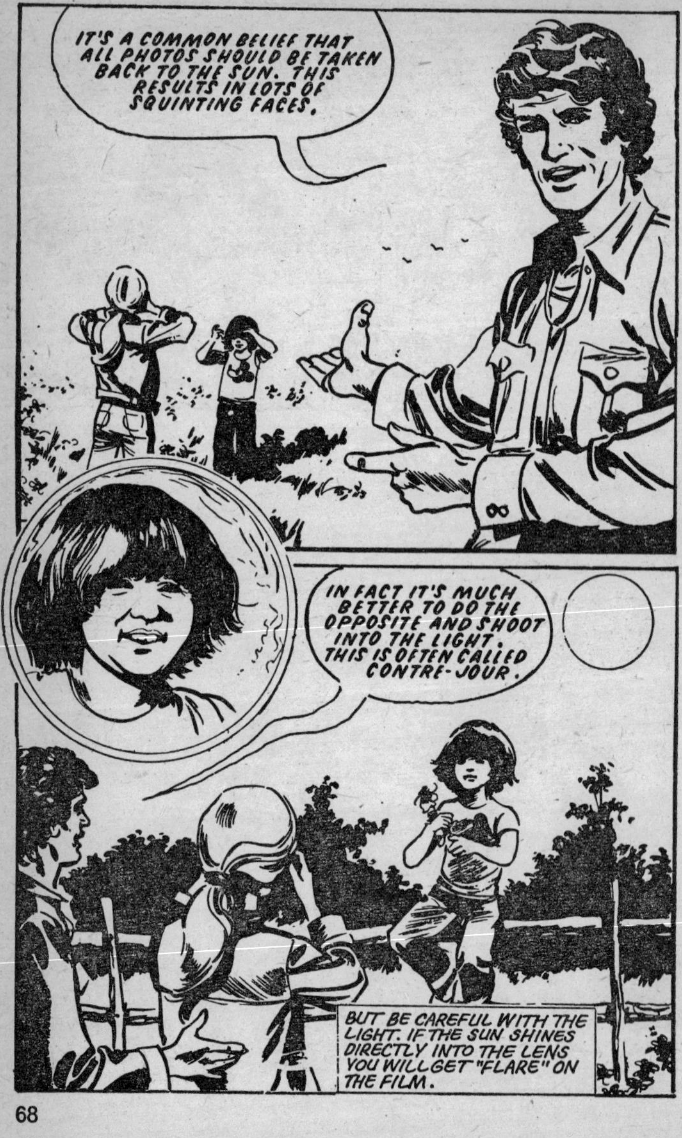

How much light in your eye?

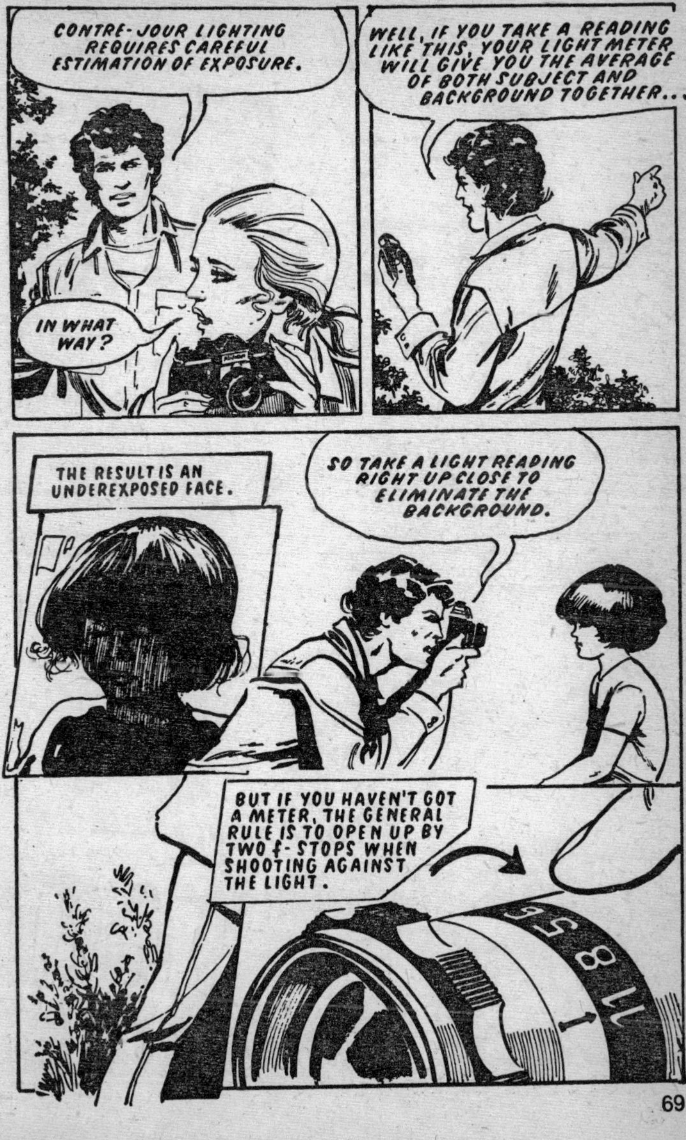

Where to use flash

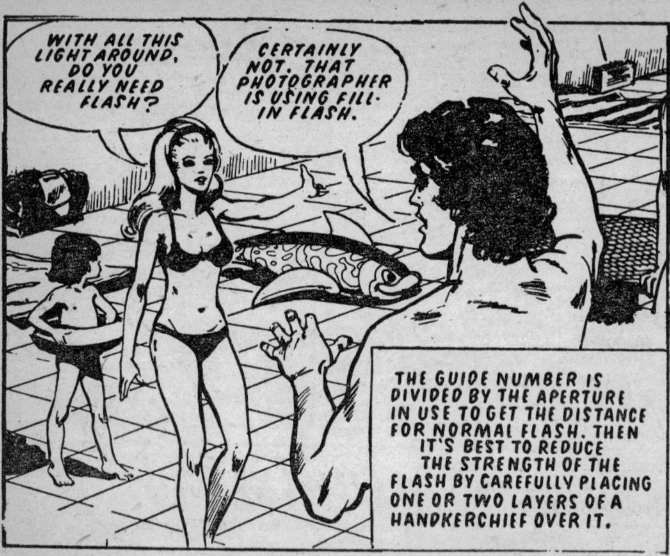

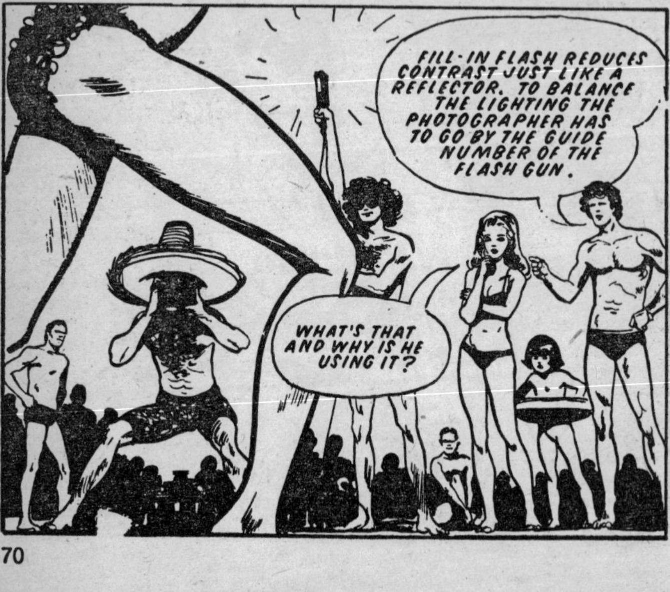

What's the best angle?

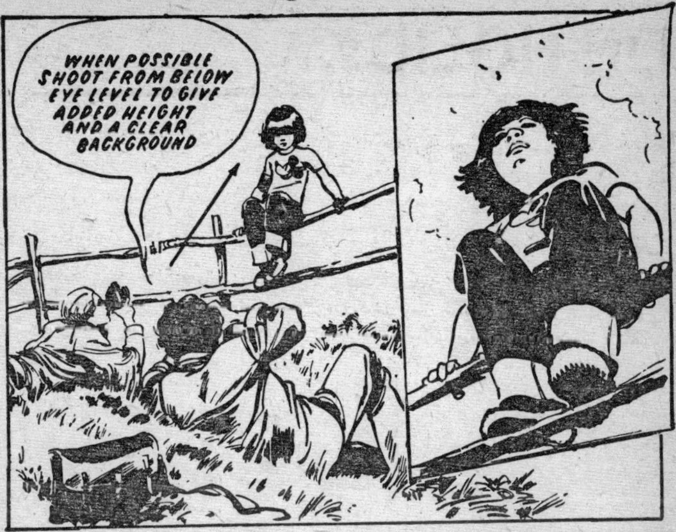

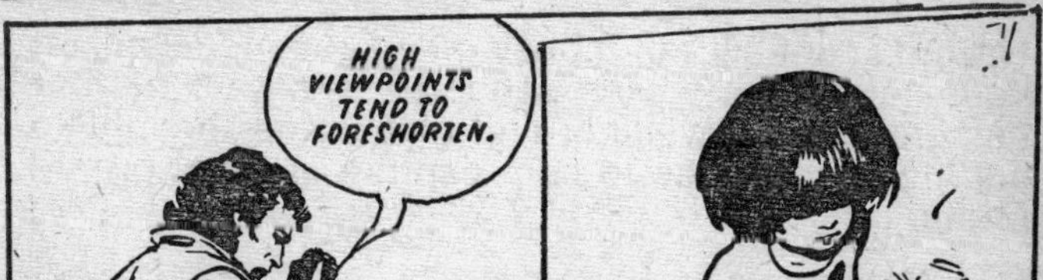

Chapter 9

ON HOLIDAY

Having spent a lot of money on your camera (and on your holiday), it makes sense to take care of your camera while travelling, and give some thought to adding accessories to help capture unusual or rare shots.

Beware of camera enemies

Vibration can loosen vital parts of your camera and upset delicate meters, so choose a good camera case for your camera and all accessories you need. It should have compartments for protection and allow you to get at things quickly.

Heat and humidity are camera-killers. Keep the camera where it is coolest — never in the car glove compartment or rear window. Keep it out of sight and locked away too, when it is not with you, and don't forget to insure it adequately.

Corrosion from seawater can ruin a camera competely. Obviously you won't drop it in the sea, but be wary of flying spray. In hazardous conditions it is worth wrapping the camera in a plastic bag with just the lens protruding. This guards against sand as well; a few particles can spoil delicate movements.

Never pack your camera or film in your main luggage when flying, if subjected to high-dose X-ray search machines the film might be fogged. Ask for a hand search, as the detectors at hand baggage check positions are unlikely to harm film.

What to take

If luggage space is precious or you are planning a holiday photo outfit from scratch to cover most likely shots, then an SLR with a standard lens and two others would cover most eventualities. The additional lenses could be a 28mm wide angle and a 70-210mm medium-range zoom. A safari holidaymaker might also add a longer 300m lens. Extension tubes or close-up lenses will add even more flexibility.

A tripod is useful for shooting interiors and architecture, but a more portable alternative is a mini-stand, called a table-tripod.

A selection of filters adds variety to pictures. A changing bag allows you to remove films jammed in the camera, or load film into a developing tank.

Catching the atmosphere

First find your subject. Post-cards and guide books can help you to find out the interesting sights, if you're not spending long in one place.

Search out significant details. Everybody has seen the overall view of Notre Dame, so pictures likely to get more attention would be ones of an archway carving, a gargoyle, flying buttress or a stained glass window and its details.

Look out for local colour as well as well-known sights. Show café scenes, busy markets or unusual (to the visitor) transport. Above all, take lots of shots of people, as well as places. To catch them naturally, shoot from a distance with a telephoto lens. From nearer at hand, shoot from the hip, especially with a wide-angle lens.

Tricky interior shots

Tripods or flashguns are often barred in historic buildings or cathedrals to avoid obstruction and encourage commercial photo sales! You can get round the problem with a table tripod, or try pressing the camera against a pillar, pew or similar support and make the exposure by using the delayed-action device, thus avoiding shutter release jogging.

In interiors such as churches, there may be a great deal of contrast between areas near windows and elsewhere, so it's worth bracketing exposures. Take one at the indicated exposure, and other shots at exposure one or two stops more and less than indicated. Do this for any worthwhile shot, as it's a small extra expense for interesting results.

Successful sunsets

Nobody can resist a sunset shot. They succeed best if you have a dominant shape — a building, yacht masts or palm trees — silhouetted against the blazing sky. They are very effective too, if there is a good cloud formation present, especially if the setting sun is filtering through.

Be careful to avoid over exposure. A straightforward reading will be all right with watery sunsets, but for the more fiery variety, shoot at one or two stops less than indicated.

Before you go

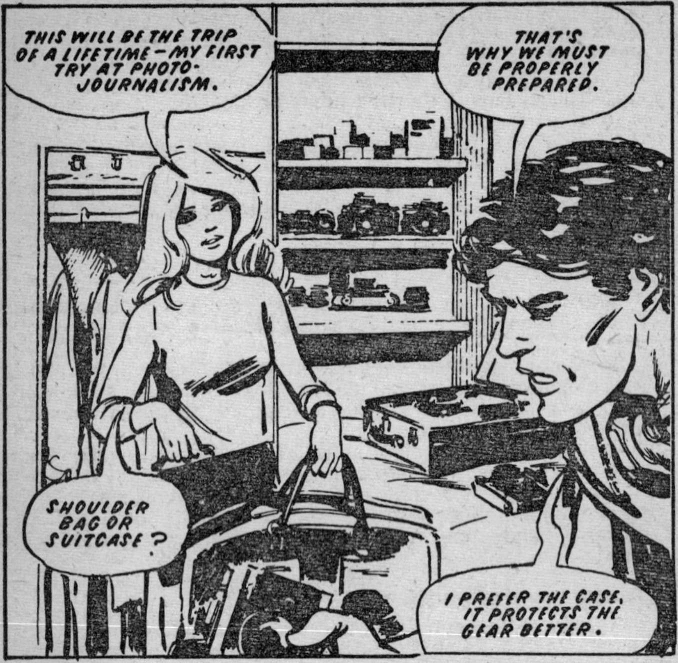

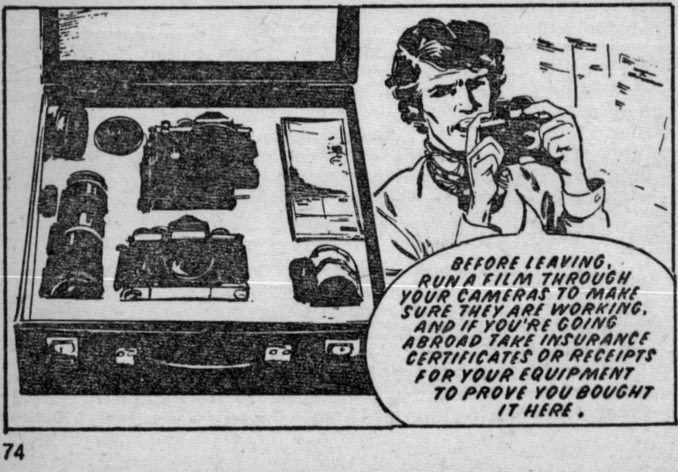

What to carry

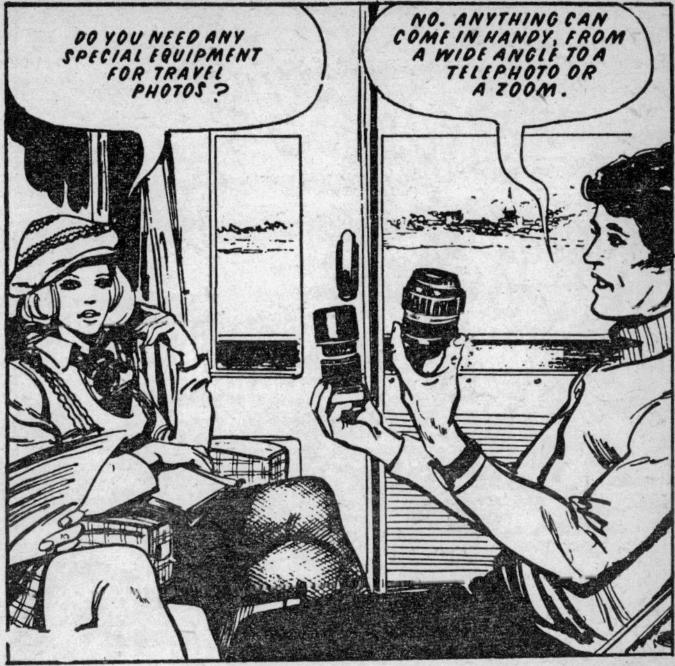

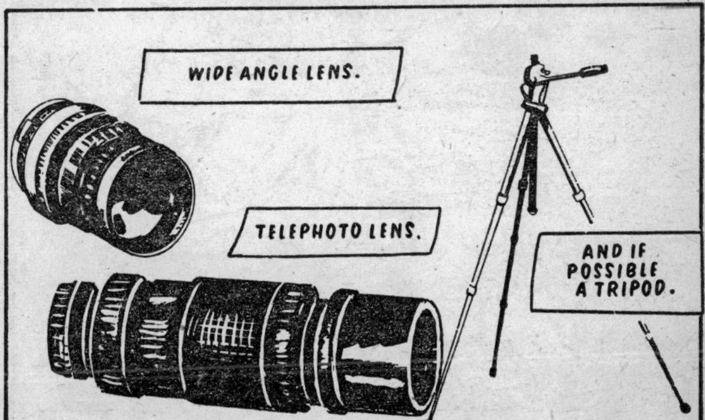

Pack the gadget bag

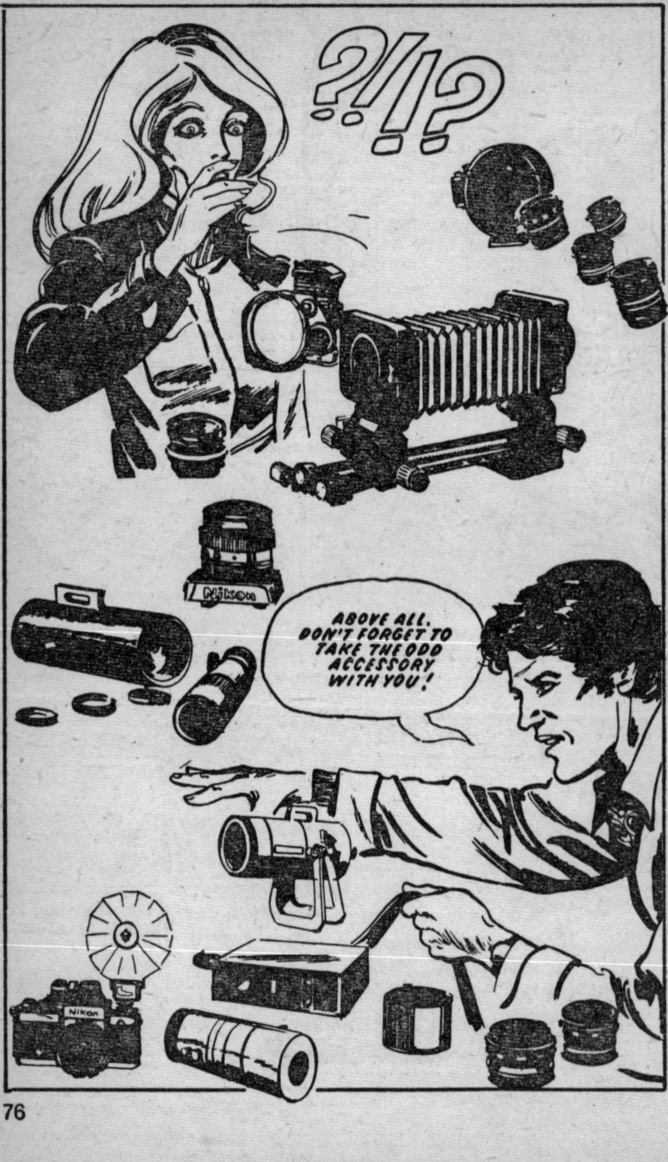

Jetting away!

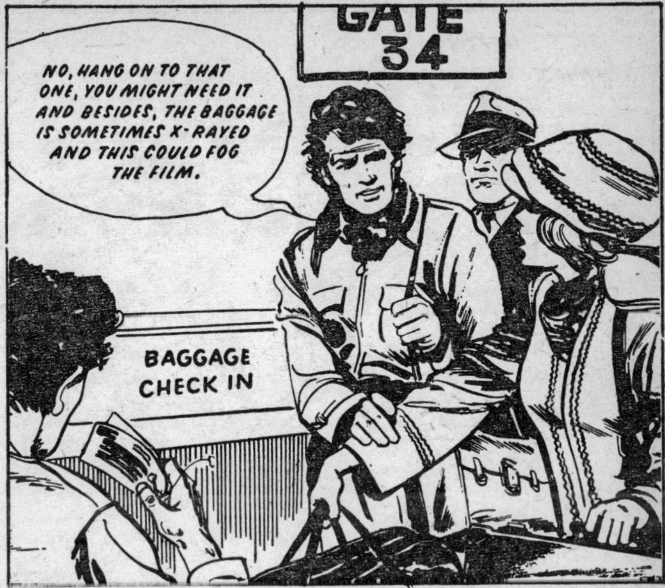

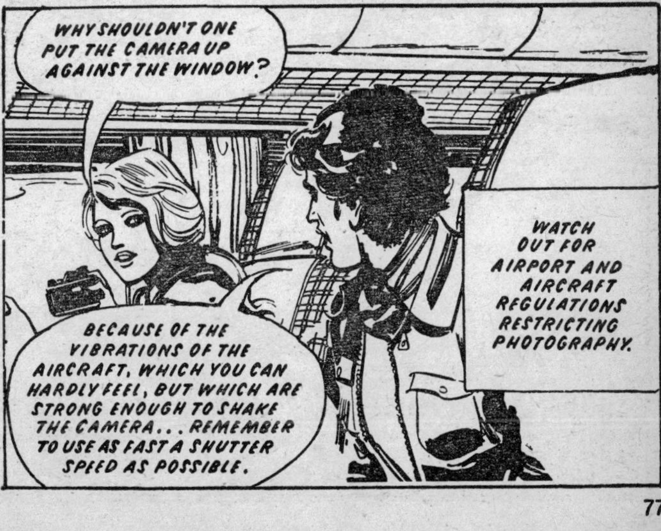

Sand, salt and sunshine

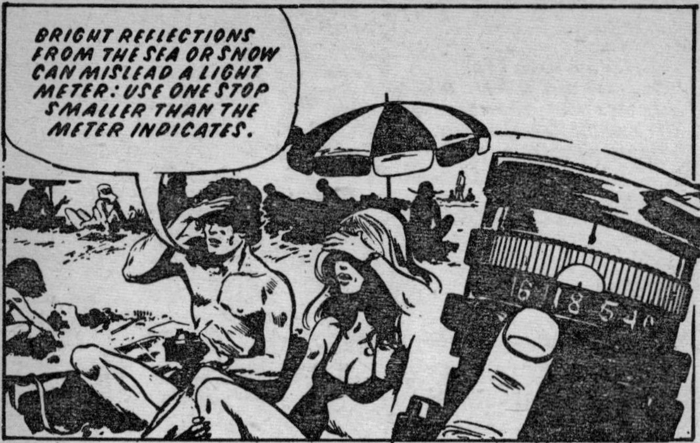

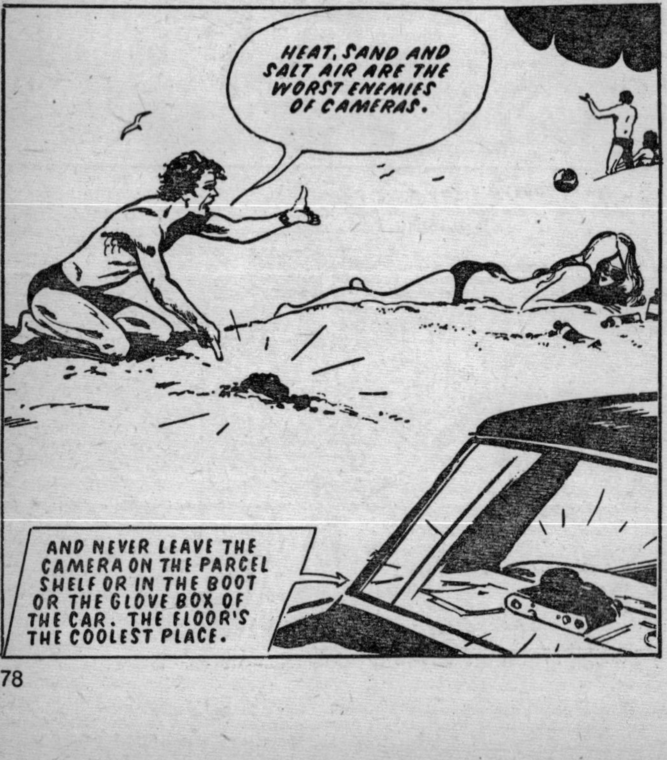

Early light, late light

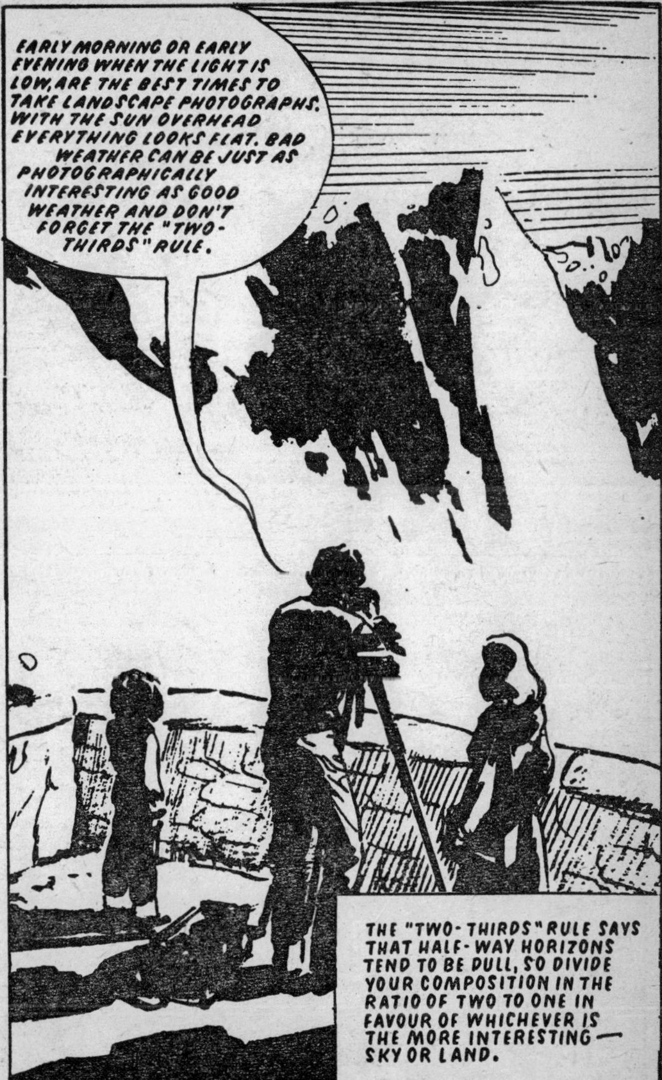

At dawn

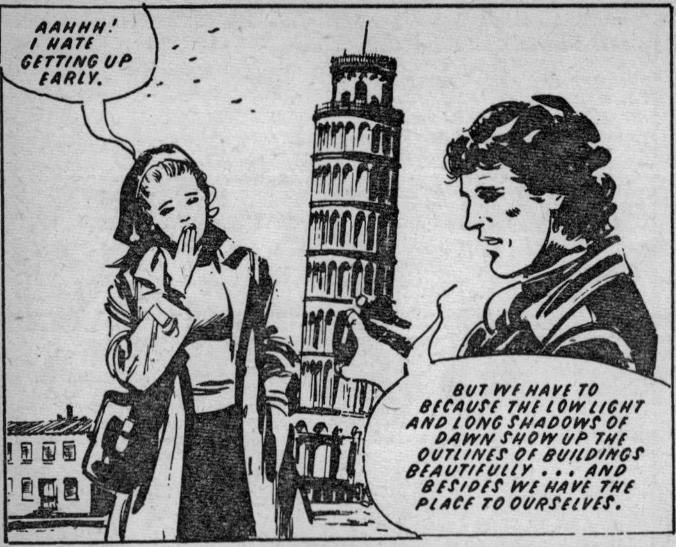
AAHHH! I HATE GETTING UP EARLY.
BUT WE HAVE TO BECAUSE THE LOW LIGHT AND LONG SHADOWS OF DAWN SHOW UP THE OUTLINES OF BUILDINGS BEAUTIFULLY . . . AND BESIDES WE HAVE THE PLACE TO OURSELVES.

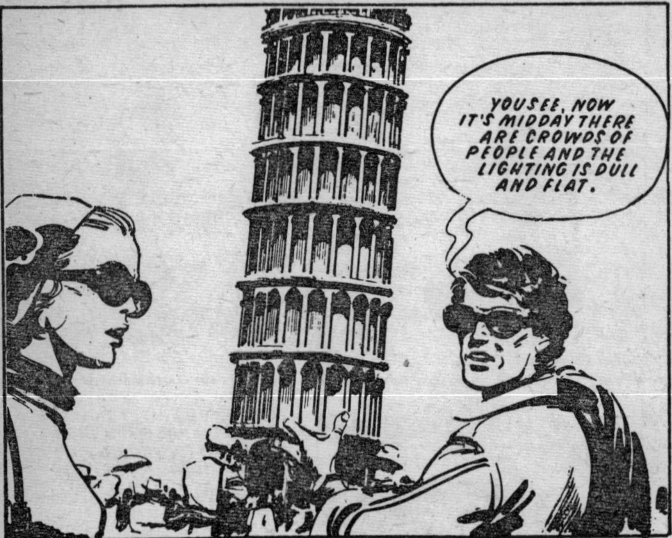
YOU SEE, NOW IT'S MIDDAY THERE ARE CROWDS OF PEOPLE AND THE LIGHTING IS DULL AND FLAT.

Original angles

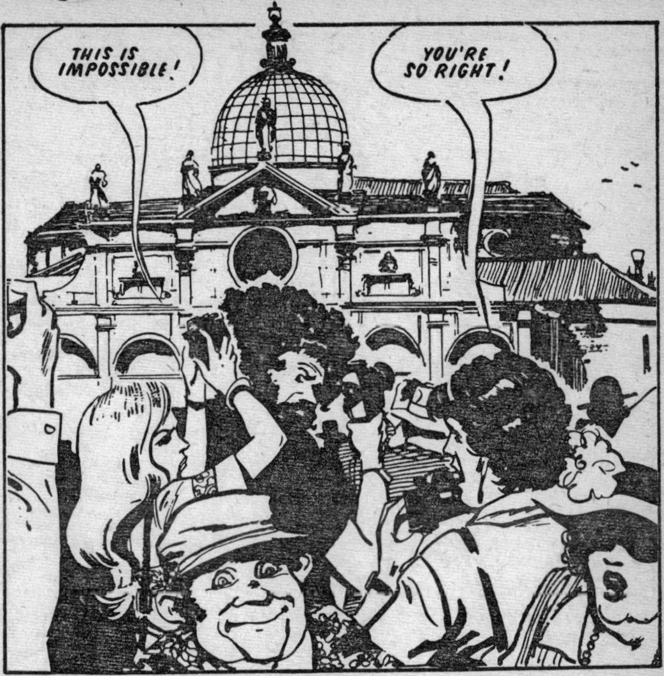

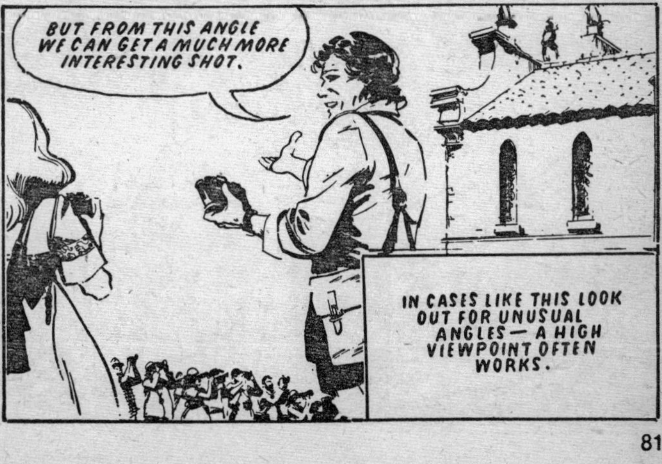

A mine of information

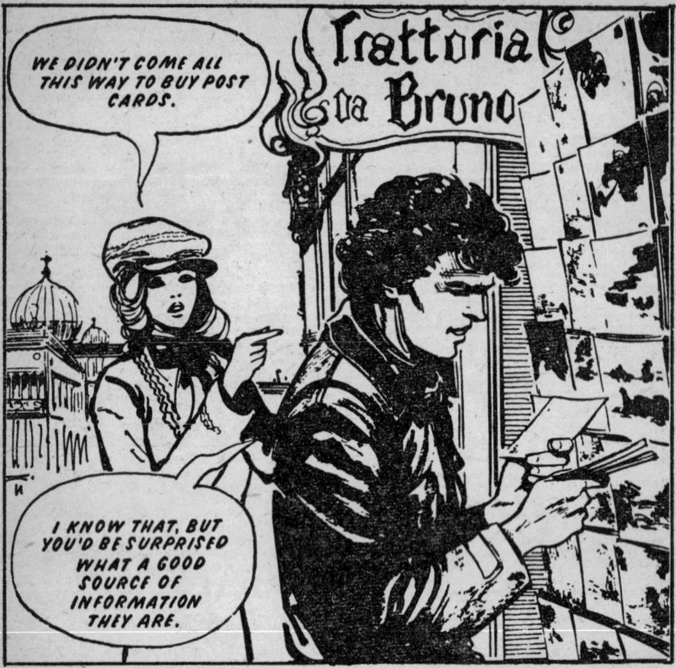

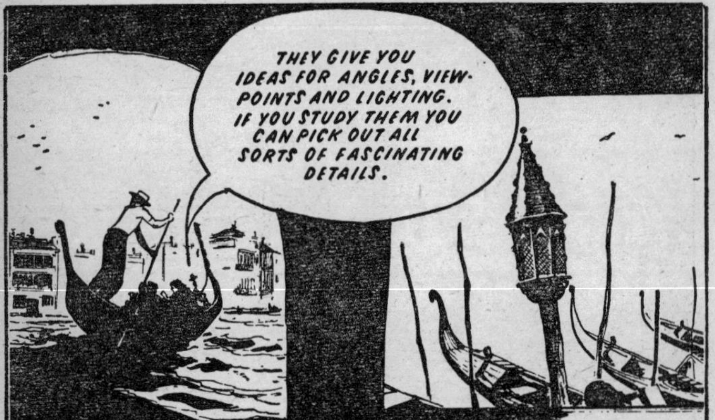

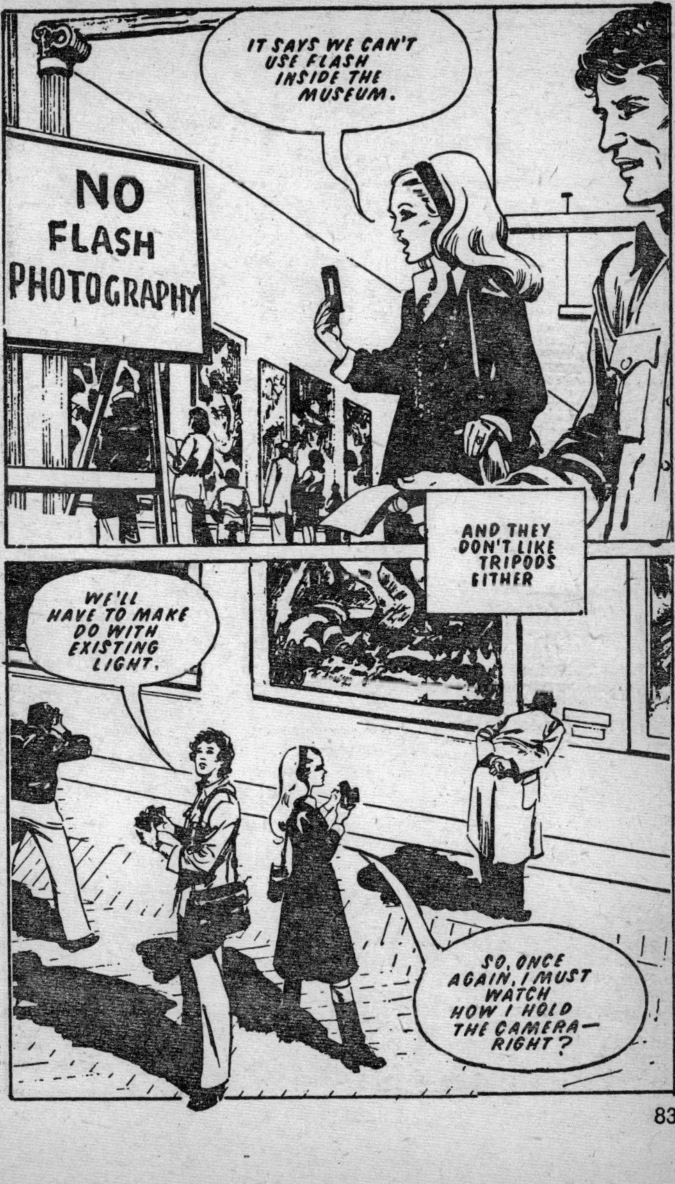
IT SAYS WE CAN'T USE FLASH INSIDE THE MUSEUM.
NO FLASH PHOTOGRAPHY
AND THEY DON'T LIKE TRIPODS EITHER
WE'LL HAVE TO MAKE DO WITH EXISTING LIGHT.
SO, ONCE AGAIN, I MUST WATCH HOW I HOLD THE CAMERA— RIGHT?

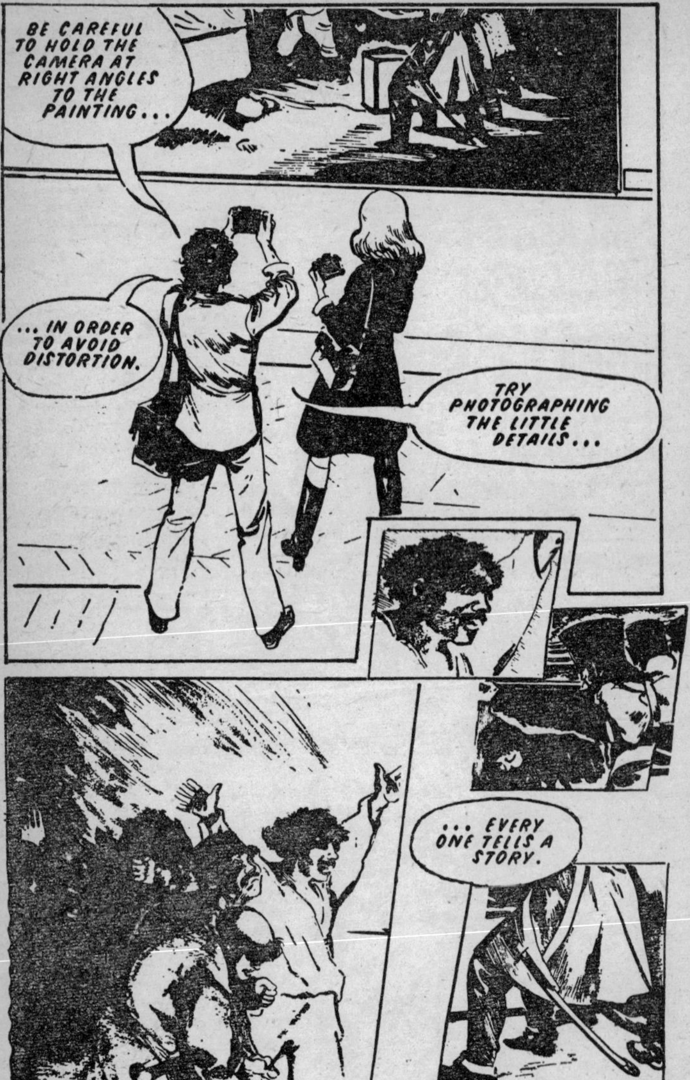
BE CAREFUL TO HOLD THE CAMERA AT RIGHT ANGLES TO THE PAINTING . . .
. . . IN ORDER TO AVOID DISTORTION.
TRY PHOTOGRAPHING THE LITTLE DETAILS . . .
. . . EVERY ONE TELLS A STORY.

Chapter 10

PHOTOS — ANYTIME, ANYWHERE

Cameras are usually bought for photographing family and friends and capturing holiday memories. But you are wasting a lot of photo opportunities if you do not use you camera for more than these enjoyable occasions.

You can use your camera to make a photo record of your other hobbies, sports and interests and you can use it to record your views of the world at large. Try thinking in terms of picture stories, not just single shots. Set yourself photo assignments. Cover a fête, or something more dramatic like a street demonstration. In the longer term, build up a pictorial record of your school, sports centre, or your locality. You don't have to travel the world for good pictures.

Photography at night and in unusual lighting is especially interesting. The table gives an idea of the sort of exposure for different situations. It can only serve as a rough guide.

Suggested settings for night exposures

Subject	Film speed 100ASA	200ASA	400ASA
Average street lighting	1/8sec at f/2.8	1/15sec at f/2.8	1/30sec at f/2.8
Brightly lit shop centres	1/30sec at f/2.8	1/30sec at f/4	1/60sec at f/4
Floodlit buildings (strong)	1sec at f/4	½ sec at f/4	¼ sec at f/4
Floodlit buildings (weak)	4sec at f/4	2sec at f/4	1sec at f/4
Exhibition hall interiors	1/15sec at f/2.8	1/30sec at f/2.8	1/60sec at f/2.8
Circus arenas	1/60sec at f/2.8	1/125sec at f/2.8	1/250sec at f/2.8
Moonlit landscape	½ sec at f/2.8	½ sec at f/5.6	½ sec at f/8
Bonfires	1/60sec at f/2.8	1/125sec at f/2.8	1/250sec at f/2.8
TV screens	1/30sec at f/2.8	1/30sec at f/4	1/30sec at f/5.6
Spotlight stage shows	1/60sec at f/2.8	1/125sec at f/2.8	1/125sec at f/4
Floodlit soccer	1/60sec at f/2	1/125sec at f/2	1/250sec at f/11
Fireworks	B at f/5.6	B at f/8	B at f/11

(Open shutter at B, camera on tripod, try apertures indicated, much depends on type and colour of fireworks).

Sail away

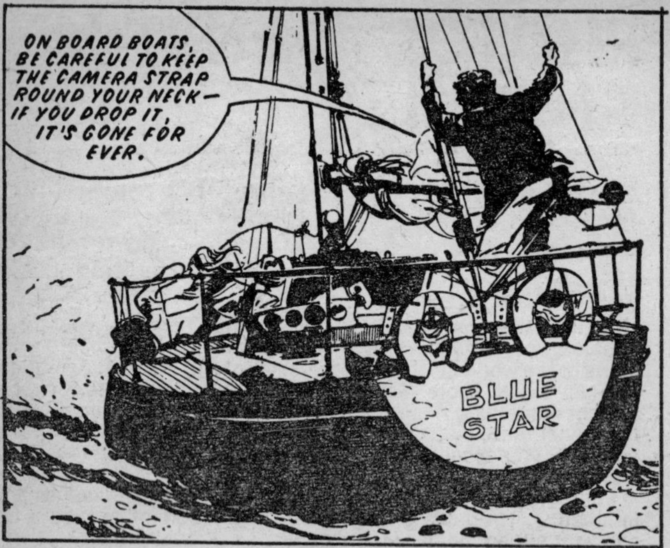
ON BOARD BOATS, BE CAREFUL TO KEEP THE CAMERA STRAP ROUND YOUR NECK – IF YOU DROP IT, IT'S GONE FOR EVER.
BLUE STAR

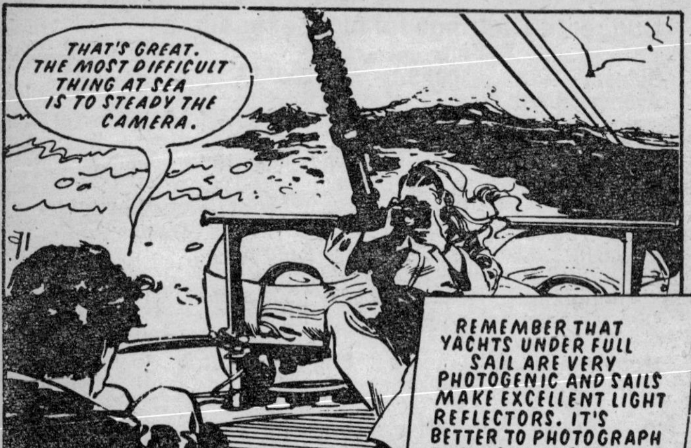
THAT'S GREAT. THE MOST DIFFICULT THING AT SEA IS TO STEADY THE CAMERA.
REMEMBER THAT YACHTS UNDER FULL SAIL ARE VERY PHOTOGENIC AND SAILS MAKE EXCELLENT LIGHT REFLECTORS. IT'S BETTER TO PHOTOGRAPH THEM OUT AT SEA THAN BETWEEN YOU AND THE LAND. AND ALWAYS USE AS FAST A SHUTTER SPEED AS POSSIBLE.

On safari

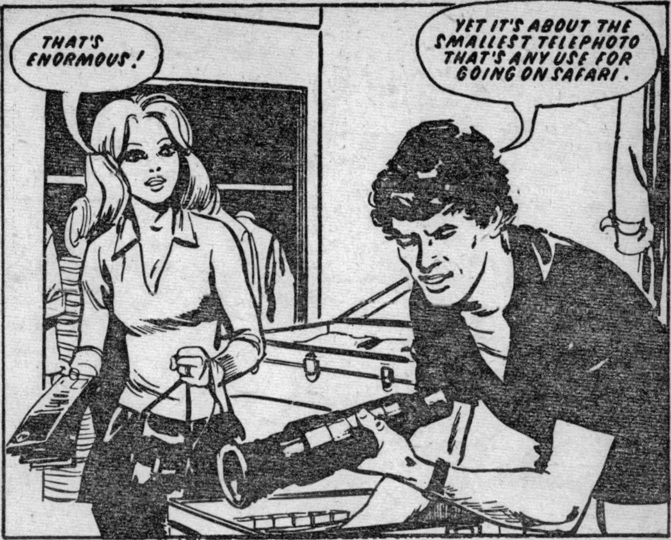

THAT'S ENORMOUS!
YET IT'S ABOUT THE SMALLEST TELEPHOTO THAT'S ANY USE FOR GOING ON SAFARI.

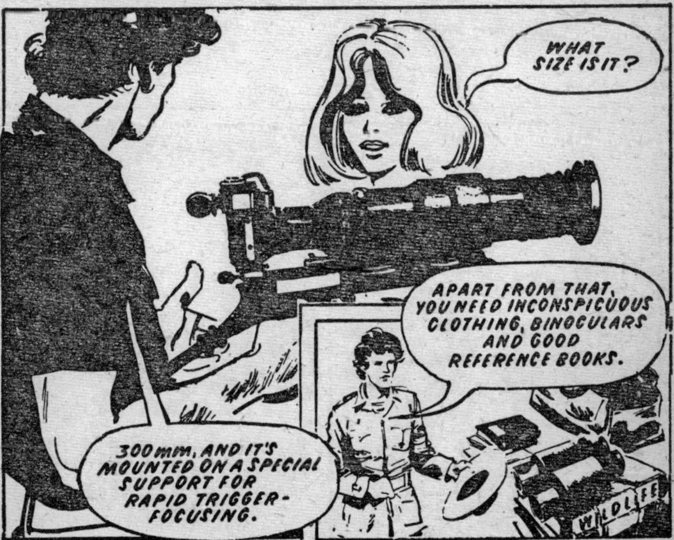

WHAT SIZE IS IT?
300mm, AND IT'S MOUNTED ON A SPECIAL SUPPORT FOR RAPID TRIGGER-FOCUSING.
APART FROM THAT, YOU NEED INCONSPICUOUS CLOTHING, BINOCULARS AND GOOD REFERENCE BOOKS.
WILDLIFE

In big game country

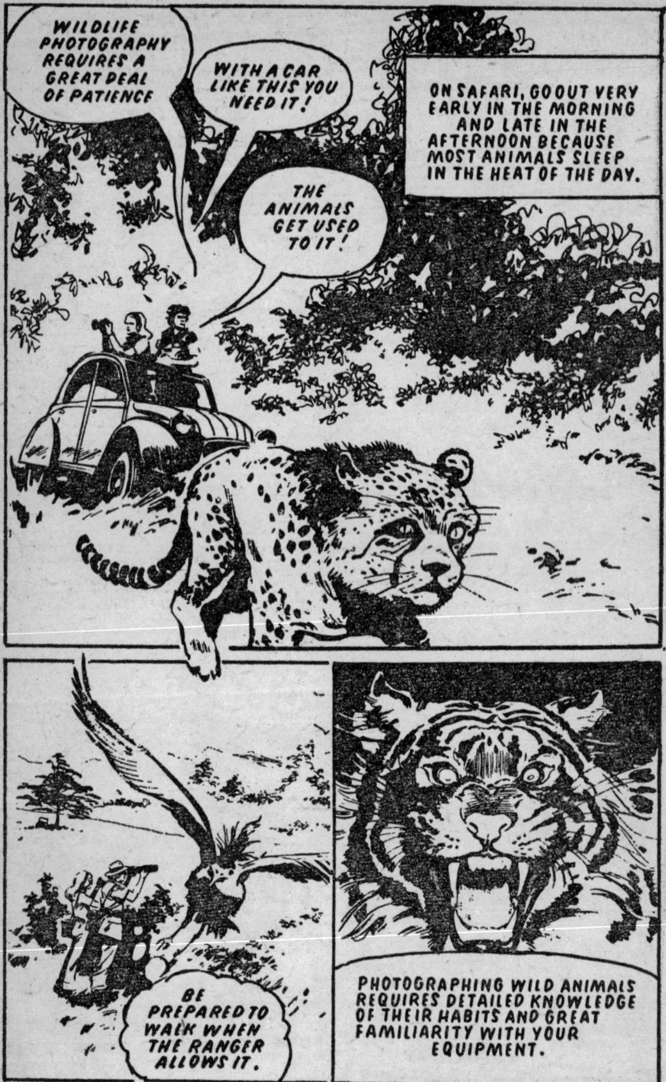

Don't catch cold

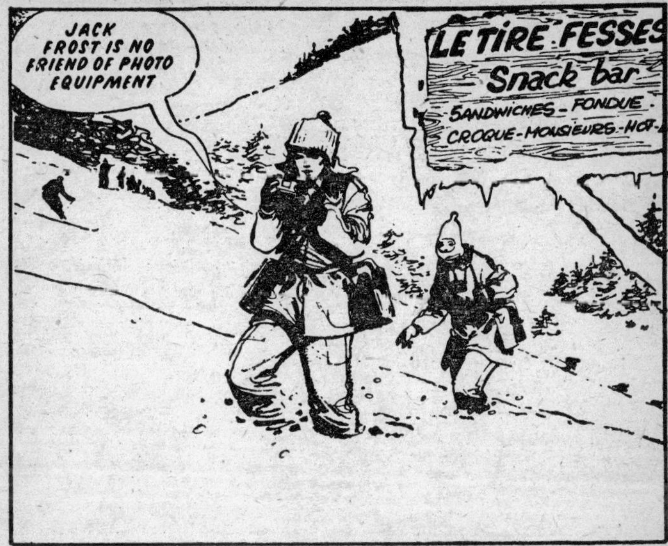

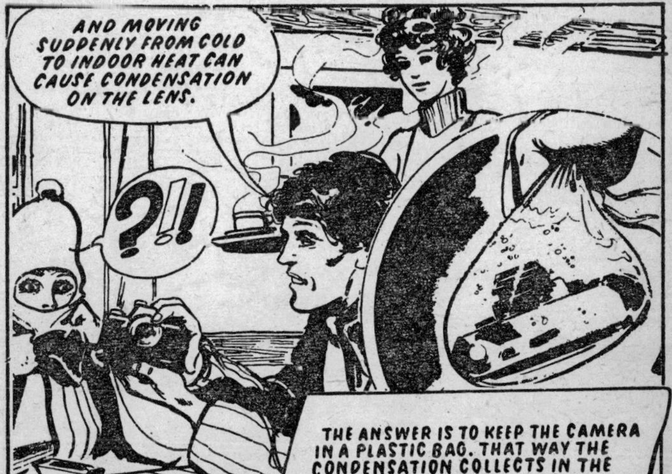

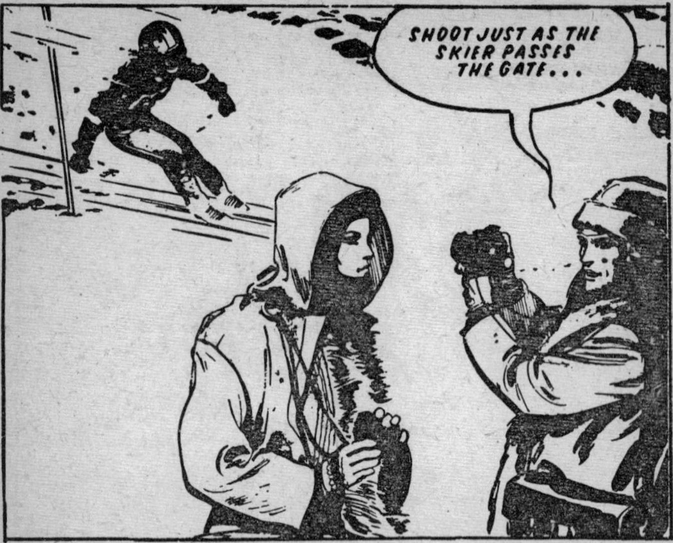
SHOOT JUST AS THE SKIER PASSES THE GATE...

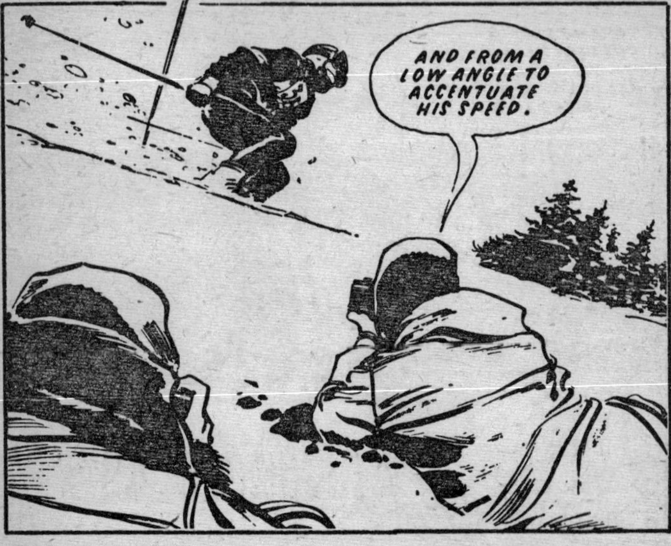
AND FROM A LOW ANGLE TO ACCENTUATE HIS SPEED.

Fast work!

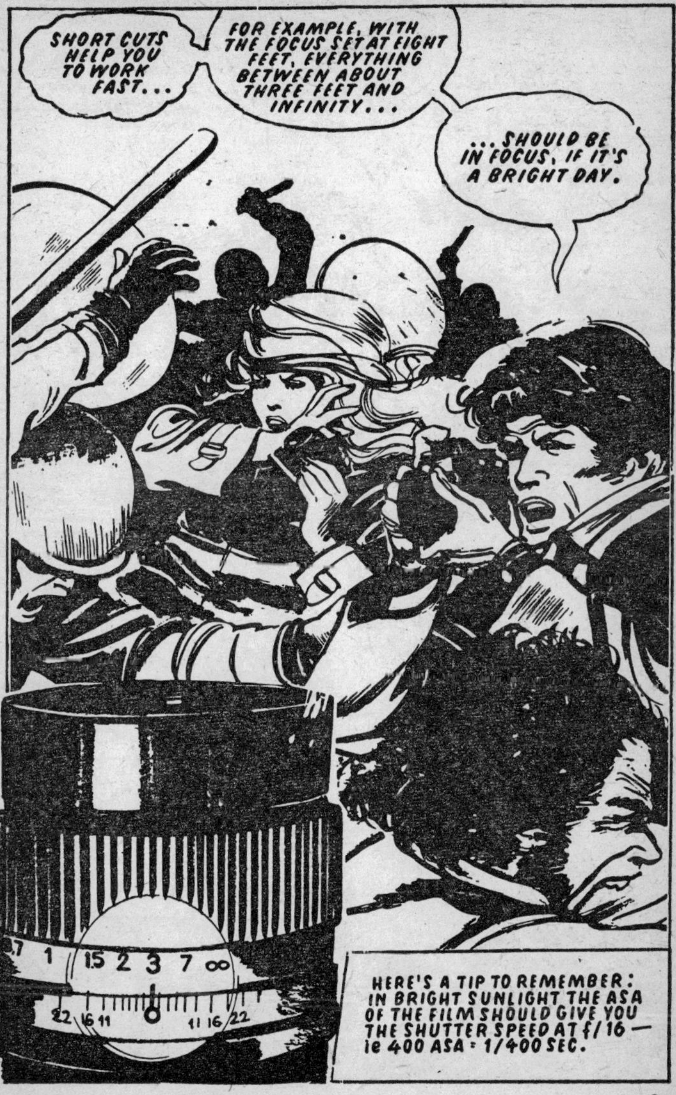
SHORT CUTS HELP YOU TO WORK FAST...
FOR EXAMPLE, WITH THE FOCUS SET AT EIGHT FEET, EVERYTHING BETWEEN ABOUT THREE FEET AND INFINITY...
...SHOULD BE IN FOCUS, IF IT'S A BRIGHT DAY.
.7 1 1.5 2 3 7 ∞
22 16 11 11 16 22
HERE'S A TIP TO REMEMBER: IN BRIGHT SUNLIGHT THE ASA OF THE FILM SHOULD GIVE YOU THE SHUTTER SPEED AT f/16 — ie 400 ASA = 1/400 SEC.

Comprehensive insurance

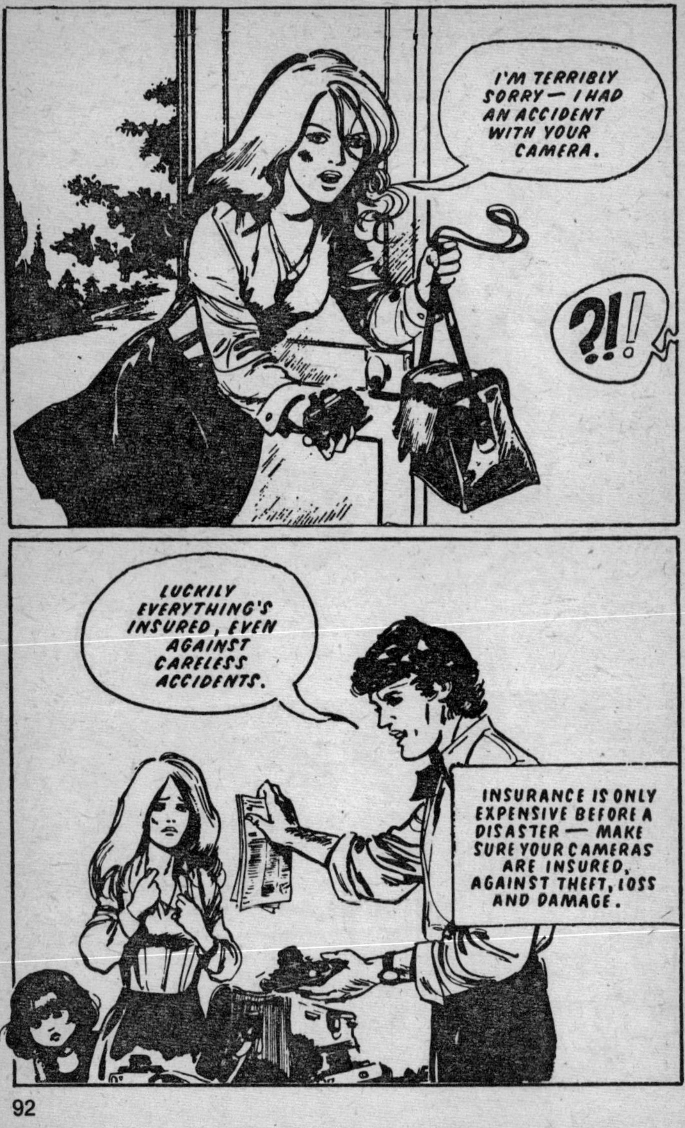

Photos after dark

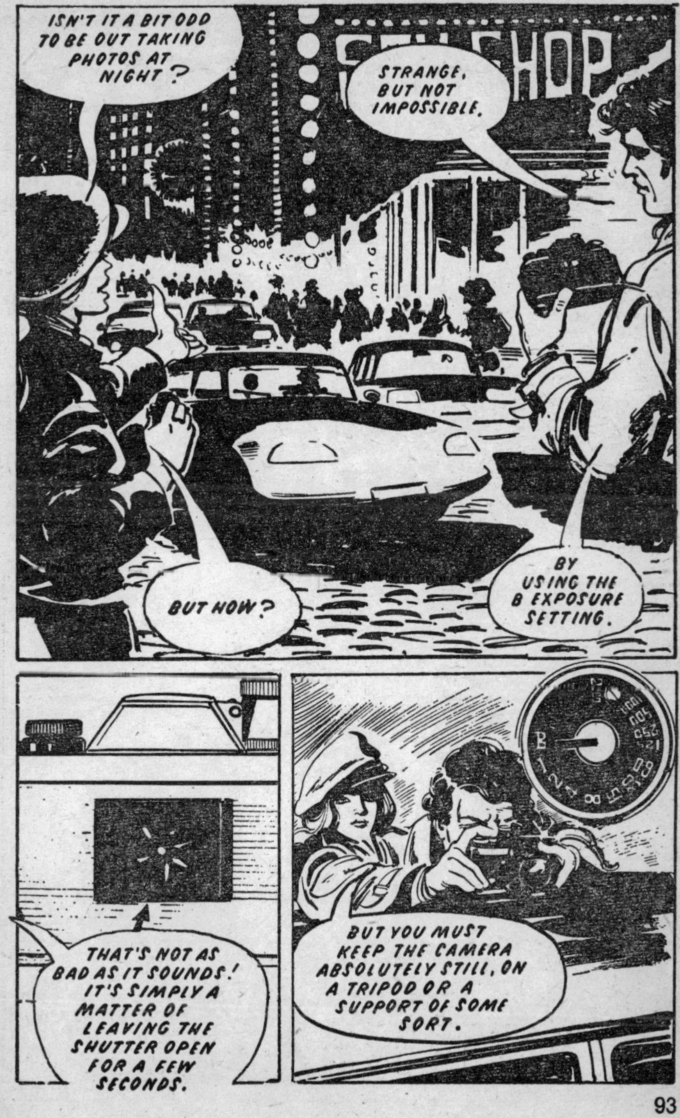

Fireworks!

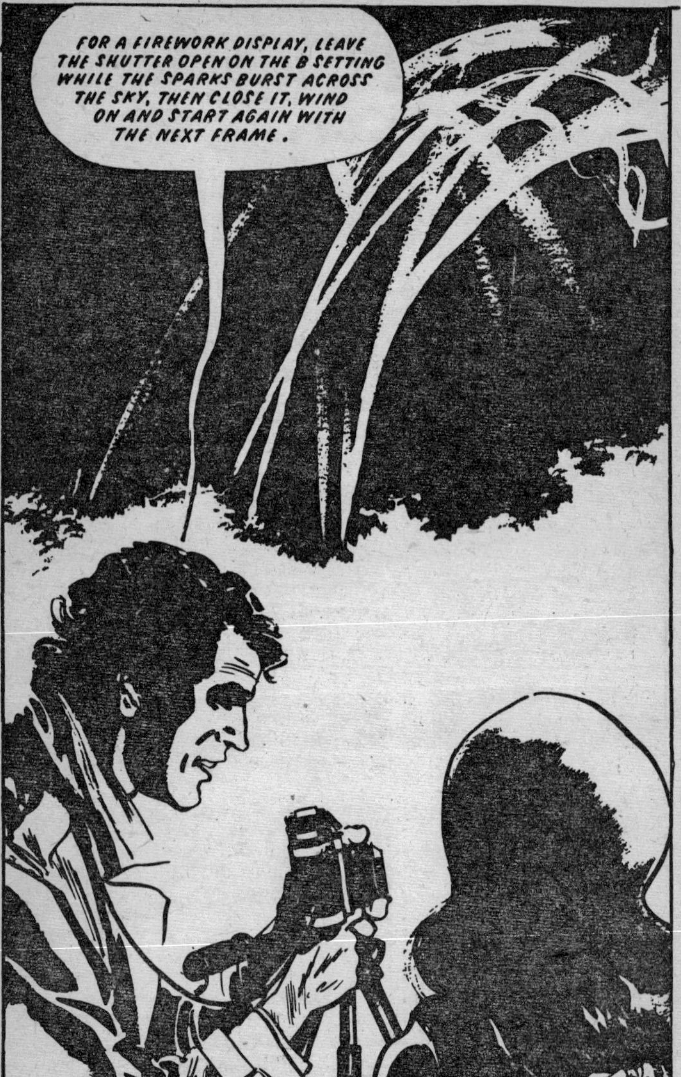
FOR A FIREWORK DISPLAY, LEAVE THE SHUTTER OPEN ON THE B SETTING WHILE THE SPARKS BURST ACROSS THE SKY, THEN CLOSE IT, WIND ON AND START AGAIN WITH THE NEXT FRAME.

Chapter 11

PHOTO ACTION

Sporting activities provide exciting photographic possibilities as do many other fast-moving subjects, but many people are put off by imagined difficulties, especially that of freezing movement.

First, don't imagine a good sports photo necessarily means that everything is very sharp. Blurred backgrounds emphasise speed.

Panning is a technique which gives a sharp image of the subject against a blurred background. For example, pick up the image of an approaching racing cyclist in your viewfinder and keep him in the centre of it by swinging your camera smoothly as he approaches. Squeeze the shutter release smoothly at the point where you want to photograph him and keep panning, like a golfer following through on his swing. With practice you should be able to get sharp images of subjects at quite slow shutter speeds.

You can freeze subjects where panning is not desirable or practical by using a fast enough shutter speed. This depends on the speed of the subject, distance from camera and whether it is passing directly across the lens or approaching obliquely. The table shows some stopping speeds.

This table enables you to see what shutter speed is required to freeze action at a distance of about 8m (25ft), with the camera held steady. Subjects further away need slower shutter speeds.

Subject	**Approach angles**		
	Subject coming straight towards the camera	Subject approaching obliquely	Subject passing across the lens
Walkers	1/30sec	1/60sec	1/125sec
Town traffic	1/60sec	1/125sec	1/250sec
Athletes	1/125sec	1/250sec	1/500sec
Cycle racing	1/250sec	1/500sec	1/1000sec
Horse racing	1/250sec	1/500sec	1/1000sec
Motor racing	1/500sec	1/1000sec	1/2000sec

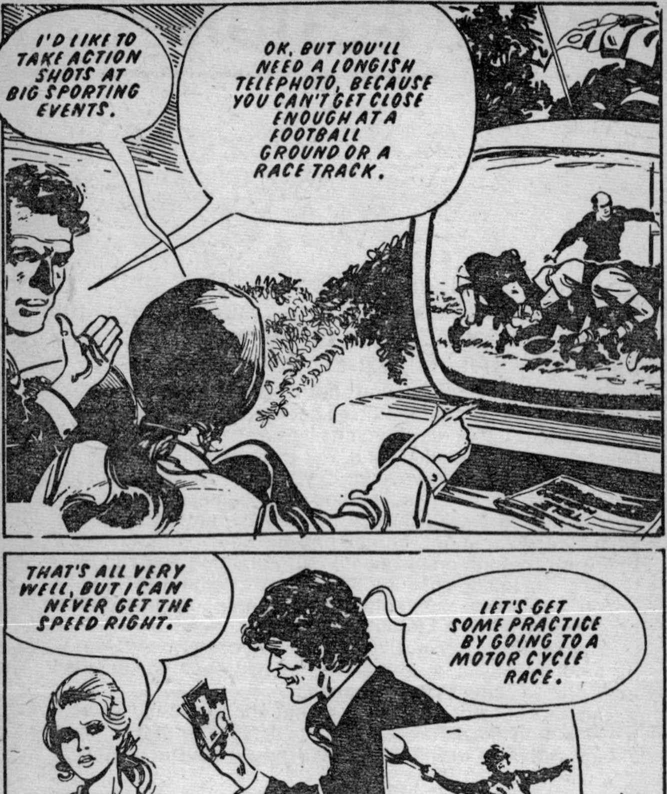
I'D LIKE TO TAKE ACTION SHOTS AT BIG SPORTING EVENTS.
OK, BUT YOU'LL NEED A LONGISH TELEPHOTO, BECAUSE YOU CAN'T GET CLOSE ENOUGH AT A FOOTBALL GROUND OR A RACE TRACK.
THAT'S ALL VERY WELL, BUT I CAN NEVER GET THE SPEED RIGHT.
LET'S GET SOME PRACTICE BY GOING TO A MOTOR CYCLE RACE.

Into action

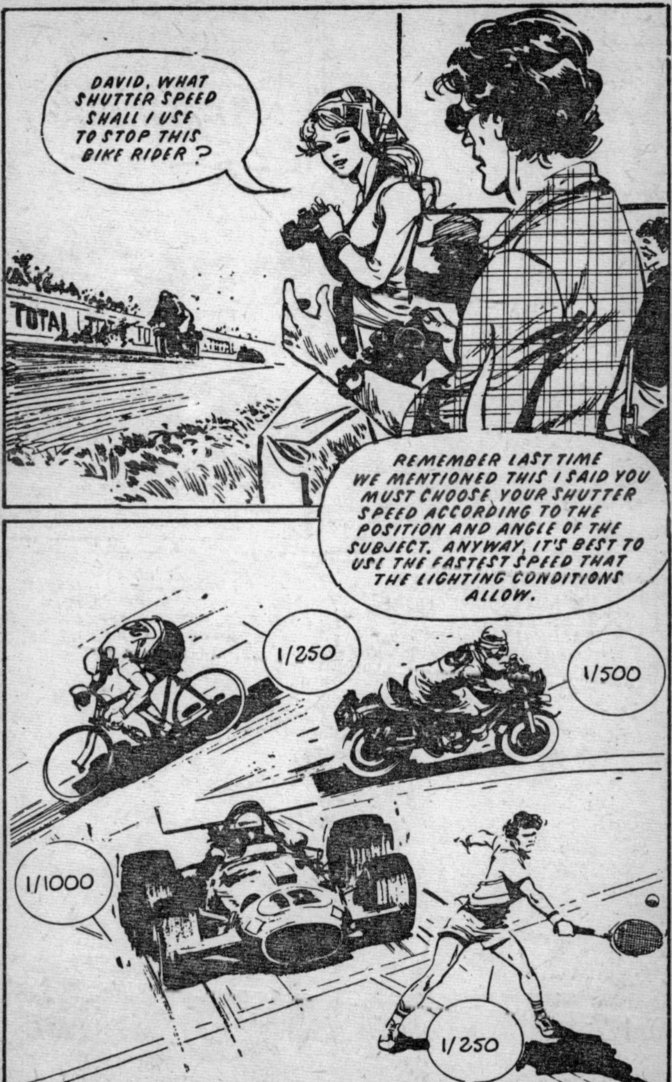
DAVID, WHAT SHUTTER SPEED SHALL I USE TO STOP THIS BIKE RIDER?
REMEMBER LAST TIME WE MENTIONED THIS I SAID YOU MUST CHOOSE YOUR SHUTTER SPEED ACCORDING TO THE POSITION AND ANGLE OF THE SUBJECT. ANYWAY, IT'S BEST TO USE THE FASTEST SPEED THAT THE LIGHTING CONDITIONS ALLOW.
TOTAL
1/250
1/500
1/1000
1/250

Panning for movement

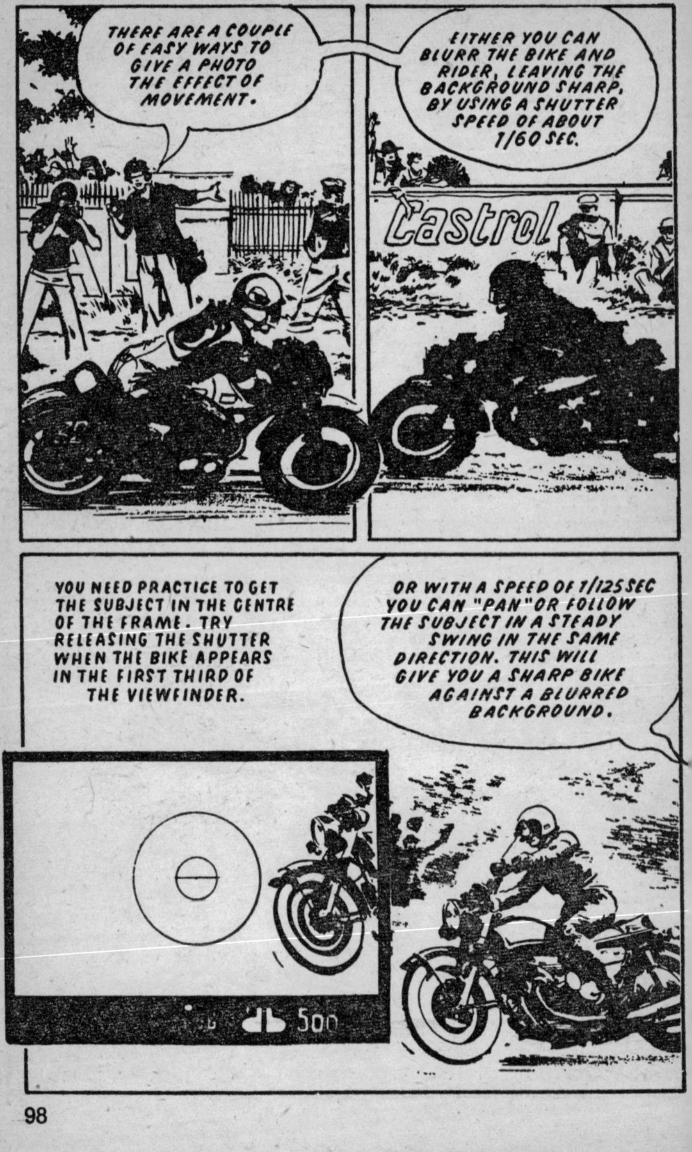

On stage

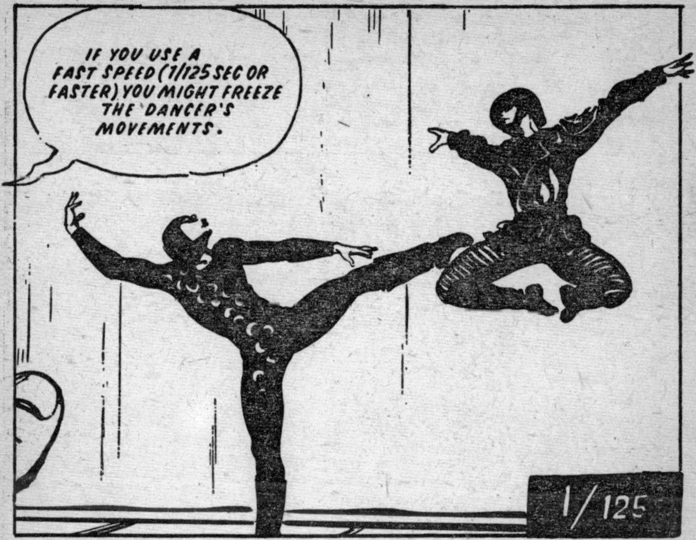
IF YOU USE A FAST SPEED (1/125 SEC OR FASTER) YOU MIGHT FREEZE THE DANCER'S MOVEMENTS.
1/125

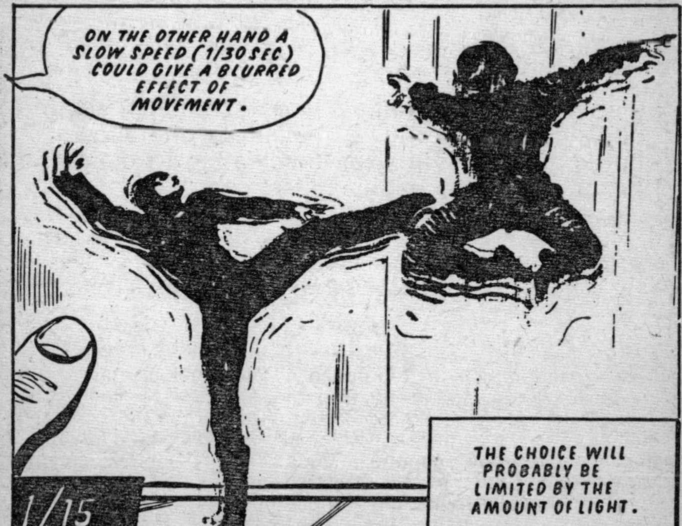
ON THE OTHER HAND A SLOW SPEED (1/30 SEC) COULD GIVE A BLURRED EFFECT OF MOVEMENT.
1/15
THE CHOICE WILL PROBABLY BE LIMITED BY THE AMOUNT OF LIGHT.

Chapter 12

ALTERING THE IMAGE

"It's very lifelike." That's a typical comment about a good photograph. But, if realism is one aspect of photography, it is just as fascinating to create an illusion and distort reality.

Special lens attachments are one eye-catching way of modifying photos. There are many types. Most are called filters. Some alter black and white photos, some colour, some both. The change is often subtle, but sets a photograph slightly apart from the average.

Filters for monochrome film

Black and white film reproduce different colours in varying shades of grey. So blue, for example, shows as a much paler shade than red. Sometimes, these contrasts can be increased deliberately. You might want a blue sky to show as a dark rather than a pale grey, so the clouds show up more clearly. Monochrome filters, usually coloured discs of thin, high-quality glass in a circular frame, change the image by restraining some colours and emphasising others. The table shows the most useful types and their effects.

Filter	Effect and uses
Yellow	Lightens yellows and light greens. Darkens blues. For landscapes, darkening blue sky slightly to emphasise clouds and make grass and foliage appear lighter.
Green	Lightens greens considerably. Darkens blues. Used as above for landscapes, especially useful if people are prominent, as skin tones are shown more naturally.
Red	Lightens reds and darkens blue considerably, showing it almost black and making skies appear very dramatic. Deeper red filters are especially effective in architectural shots.

Filters for Colour Film

The filters most commonly used with colour film are those which make the colours appear warmer, cooler, clearer, or allow films balanced for daylight or flash to give natural results in tungsten light, or vice versa.

Filter	Effects and uses
Ultra-violet (UV) (also useful with monochrome film)	Cuts out ultra-violet (invisible) light, giving clearer colours, especially in the mountains and near the sea.
Skylight (also useful with monochrome film)	Compensates for excess blueness on cloudy days, giving warmer result.
Polarising	Eliminates reflections and glare by cutting down polarised light, like sunglasses. Deepens blue skies.
Conversion	Allows film balanced for one type of light to be used in another (*eg.* daylight to artificial light).

UV, Skylight and Polarising filters can also be used with black and white film.

Special effects filters

Seductive, striking or bizarre modifications can be made to colours by means of special filters. The names usually indicate the effect: soft focus; fog; multi-image; starburst; diffraction; graduated (so that only half the picture is filtered or coloured); centre spot (clear centre, tinted surrounds).

Most of these types are easily available and relatively cheap. Descriptive brochures of the well advertised brands give a surprising amount of information.

Magic filters

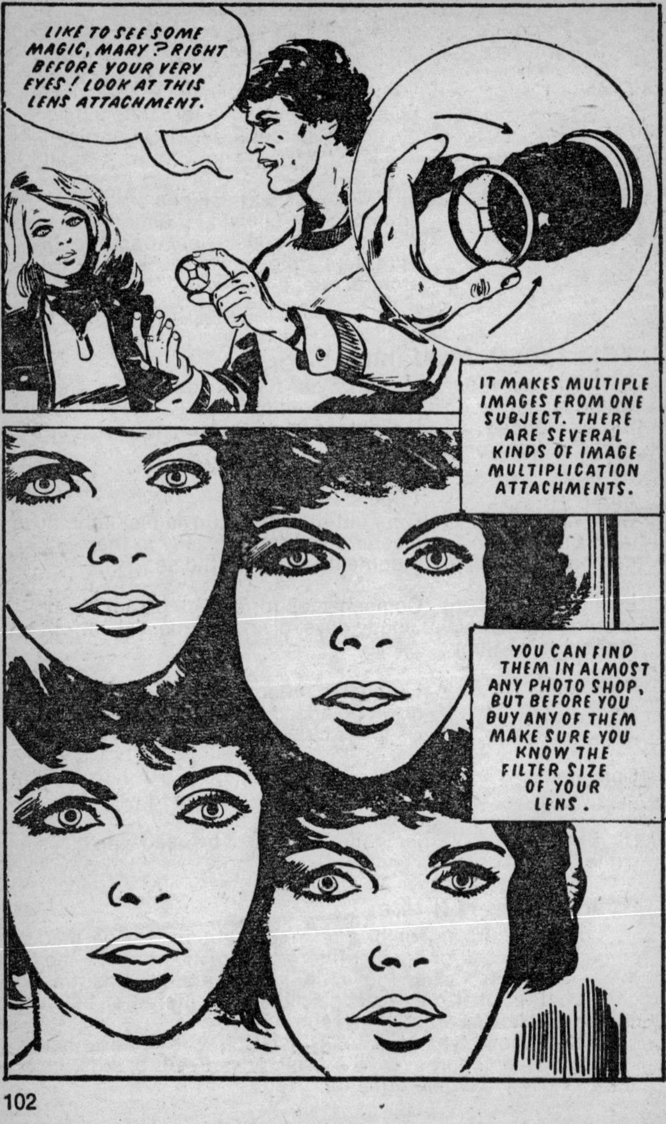

Doubling up

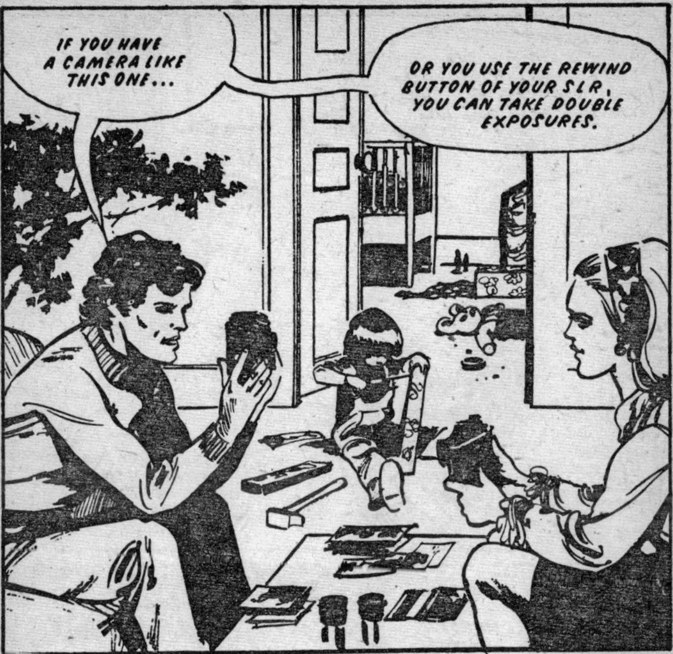
IF YOU HAVE A CAMERA LIKE THIS ONE...
OR YOU USE THE REWIND BUTTON OF YOUR SLR, YOU CAN TAKE DOUBLE EXPOSURES.

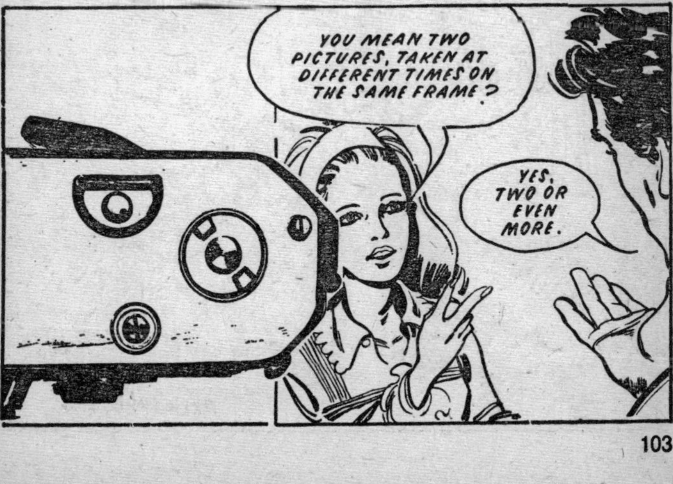
YOU MEAN TWO PICTURES, TAKEN AT DIFFERENT TIMES ON THE SAME FRAME?
YES, TWO OR EVEN MORE.

Effective double exposures

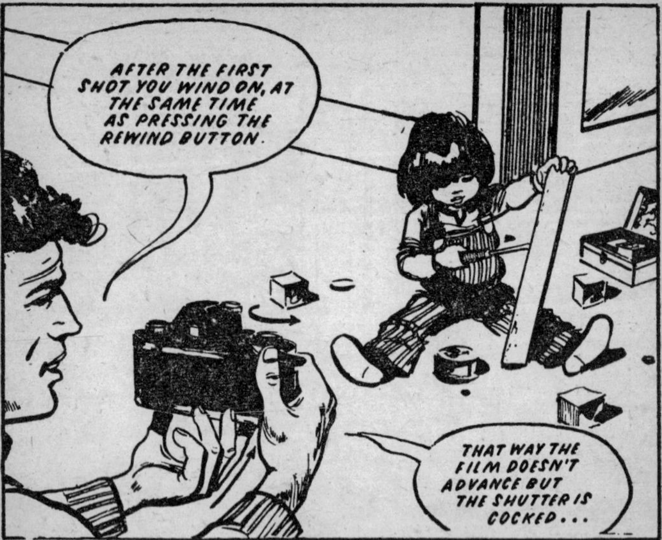

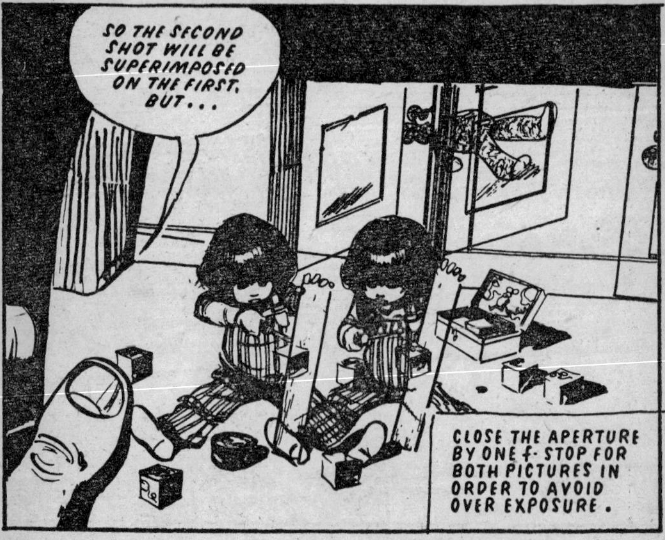

Create with infra red

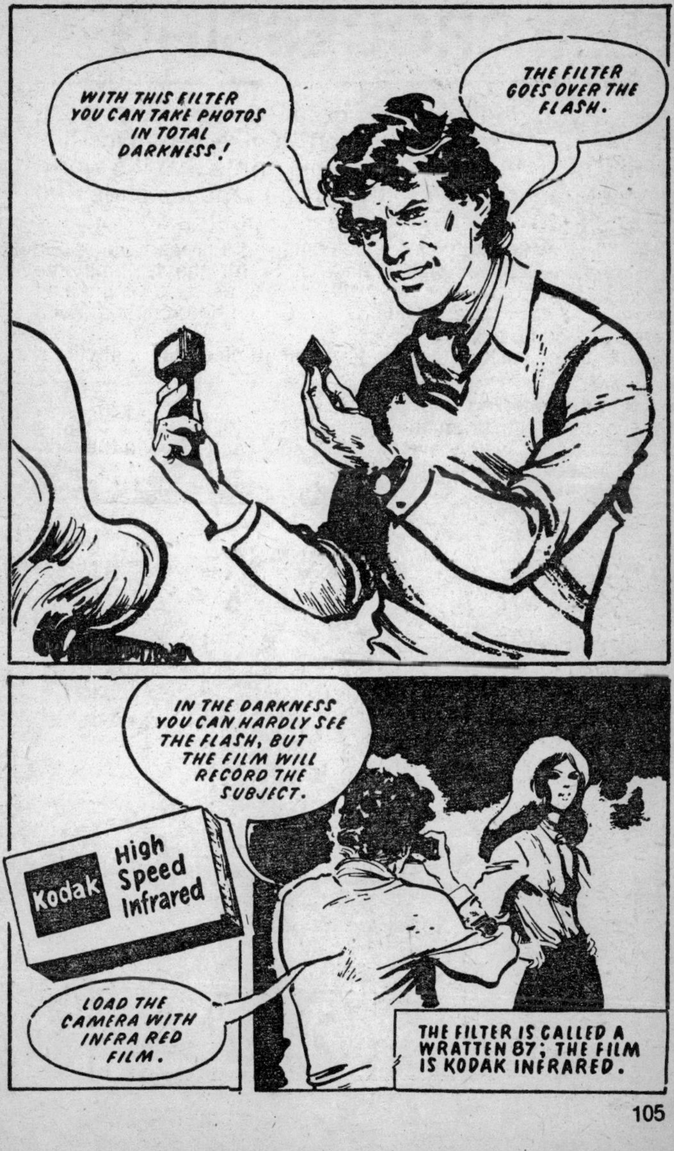

Chapter 13

FILM PROCESSING

Even if you don't want to go in for darkroom work, the way the film is processed to give negatives has such a big influence on the final prints that it's worth at least understanding it. You can process slide film yourself too, which cuts down the cost of colour.

For film developing you do not even need a properly equipped darkroom, just a completely dark place for the few minutes needed to load the film into the developer tank. You could temporarily black out the window, use a light-tight cupboard or a special changing bag.

Here are the basic stages for developing a black and white film:

In darkness

1. **Load developing tank**
   Free the film from the cassette, cartridge, or roll backing paper, then wind it evenly onto a spiral and place in the tank. Screw on the light-tight lid.

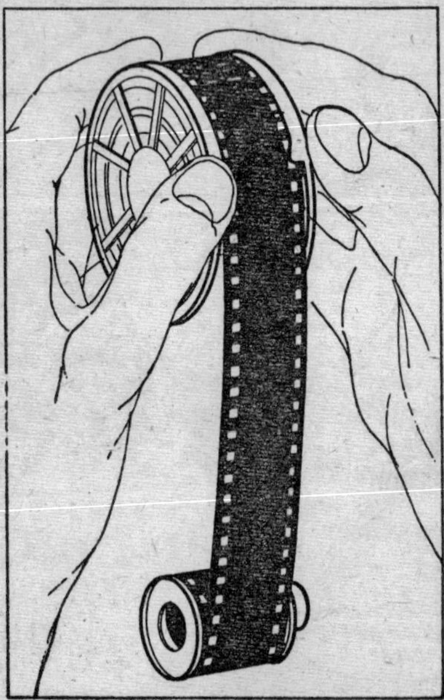

Loading an exposed film into a developing tank spiral. This must be done in total darkness.

All other stages done in the light

2. **Prepare chemicals**
   You'll need: film developer, diluted as per instructions, rinsing water (or weak stop bath acid solution) and fixer, diluted as stated. Also: graduated containers and an accurate thermometer.
3. **Pour in film developer**
   It must be at the recommended temperature: 20°C (68°F)
4. **Time, agitate, check temperature**
   Developer is left in for a specified time, around 10 minutes is usual. To avoid unevenness, tank must be agitated by inverting it at regular intervals. Keep the temperature constant.
5. **Pour out developer**
   Some types are saved for re-use, some are used only once.
6. **Pour in stop-bath rinse**
   About 20 seconds is sufficient. This and next bath should be near 20°C (68°F) too.
7. **Fix film**
   Rapid type fixers are best, they only take about a minute. Fixer is re-used, but not too often — see intructions on bottle.
8. **Wash the film**
   Still in tank, leave for about 20 minutes in fast-running water, or several complete changes.
9. **Wipe and dry**
   Unwind the film from spiral very carefully — it's delicate when wet. Swab with film wiper, hang and dry in a dust-free area. When bone dry, it is ready for cutting into strips, then for printing.

Which developer?

Liquid film developers ready for dilution are most convenient. Use a general-purpose type first. Later you can experiment with types that increase the speed of the film, or give greater resolution or finer grain.

Pushing the film

You can expose a complete roll of film at a faster speed rating (say 800ASA instead of 400ASA — that is pushed one stop). Then you give extra development time, say a third longer, or use a speed-increasing developer. The negatives will then be dense enough for making good prints, though they may have more contrast, and more grain.

Processing slide films

The main difference from developing monochrome negative film is that more processing baths are used, though only a total of four in the simplest kits. After the first developer stage you have to reverse the image to make it positive (ready for direct viewing as a slide). This is done by exposing it to bright light, or by a chemical bath. All processing solutions must be kept at a higher temperature — typically 38°C (100°F) with very little variation permitted.

Take twins

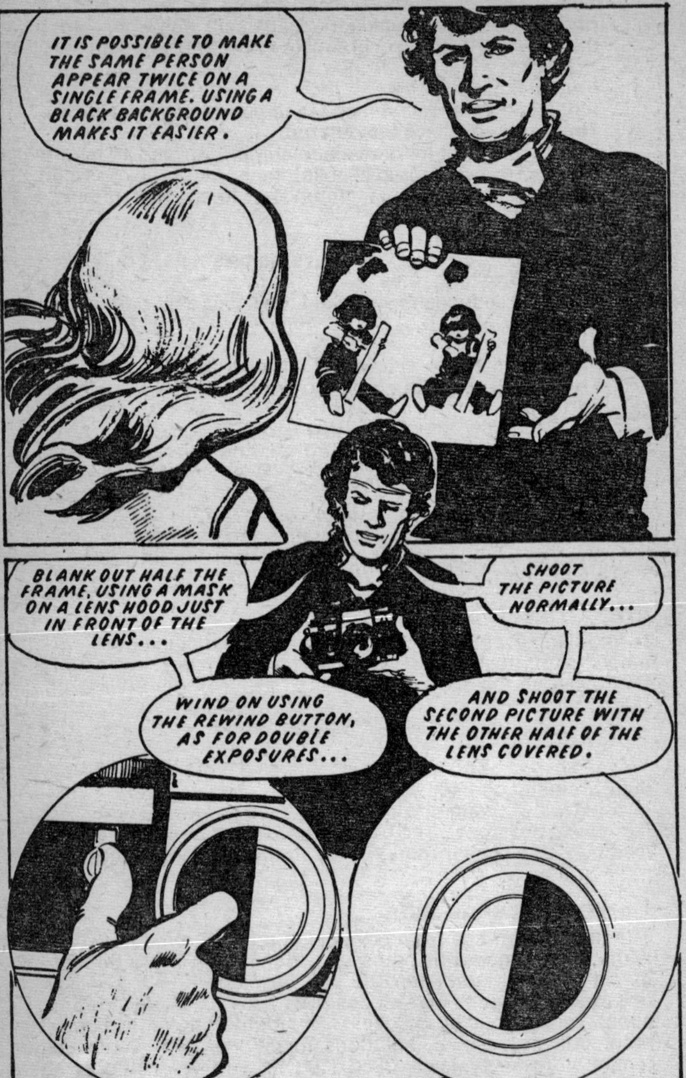
IT IS POSSIBLE TO MAKE THE SAME PERSON APPEAR TWICE ON A SINGLE FRAME. USING A BLACK BACKGROUND MAKES IT EASIER.
BLANK OUT HALF THE FRAME, USING A MASK ON A LENS HOOD JUST IN FRONT OF THE LENS...
SHOOT THE PICTURE NORMALLY...
WIND ON USING THE REWIND BUTTON, AS FOR DOUBLE EXPOSURES...
AND SHOOT THE SECOND PICTURE WITH THE OTHER HALF OF THE LENS COVERED.

Preliminary precautions

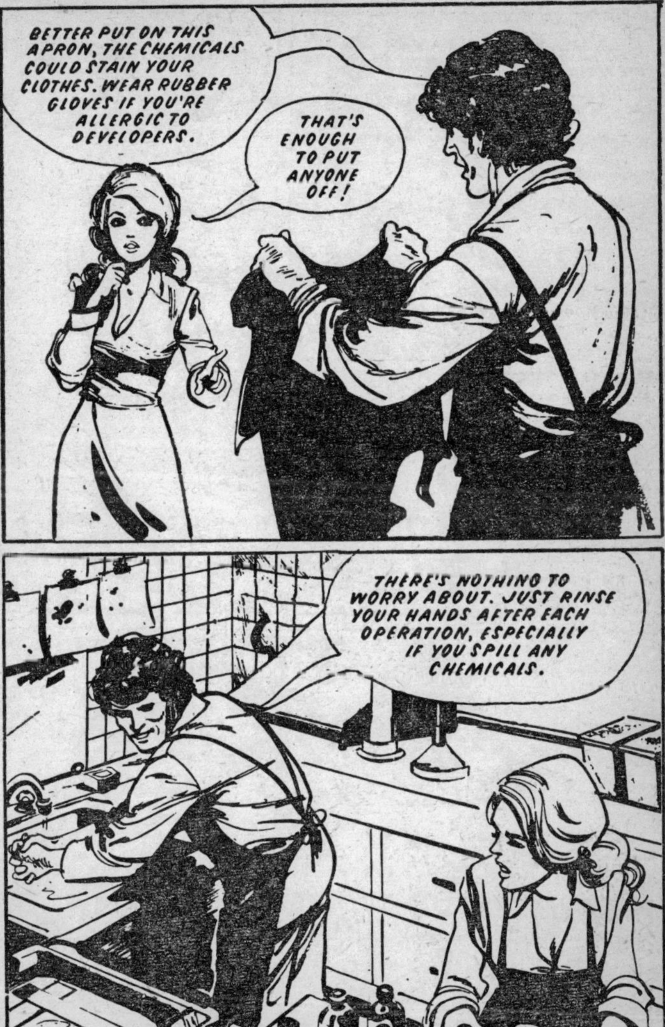

Developer

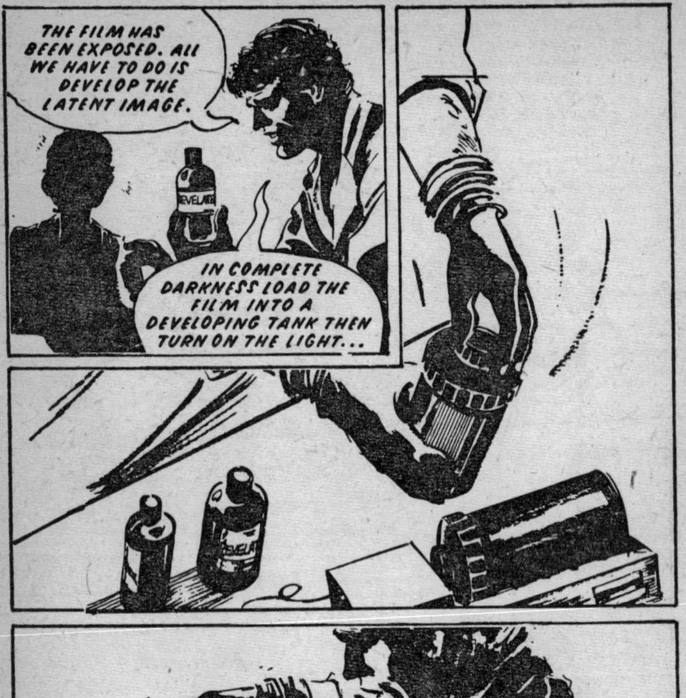

THE FILM HAS BEEN EXPOSED. ALL WE HAVE TO DO IS DEVELOP THE LATENT IMAGE.
IN COMPLETE DARKNESS LOAD THE FILM INTO A DEVELOPING TANK THEN TURN ON THE LIGHT...
POUR DEVELOPER INTO THE TANK AT THE RECOMMENDED TEMPERATURE, AND AGITATE IT FOR THE TIME GIVEN IN THE INSTRUCTIONS

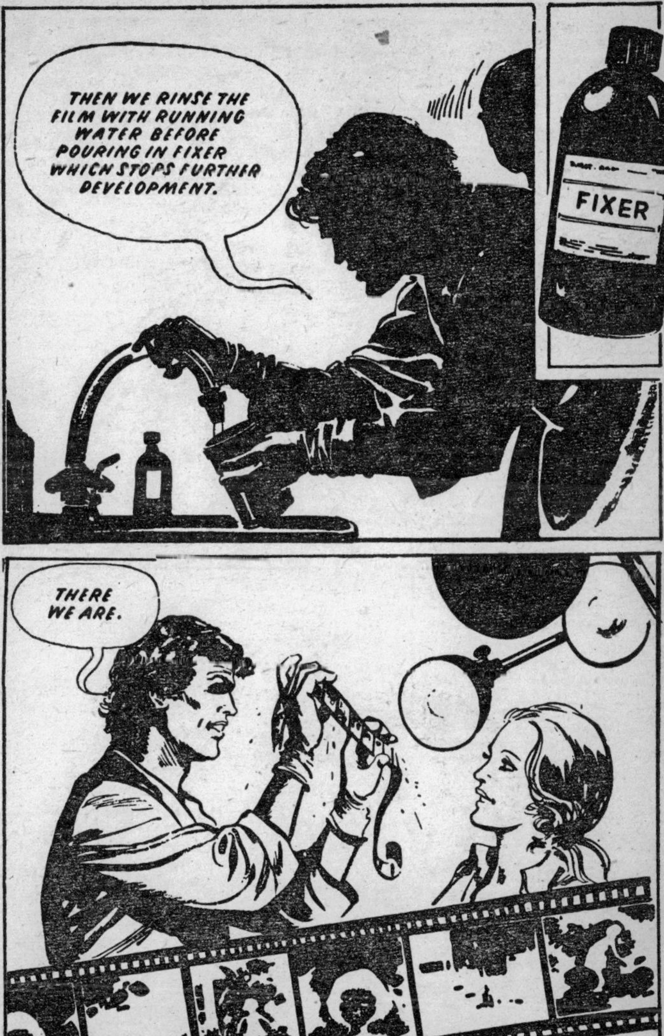
THEN WE RINSE THE FILM WITH RUNNING WATER BEFORE POURING IN FIXER WHICH STOPS FURTHER DEVELOPMENT.
FIXER
THERE WE ARE.

How to push a film

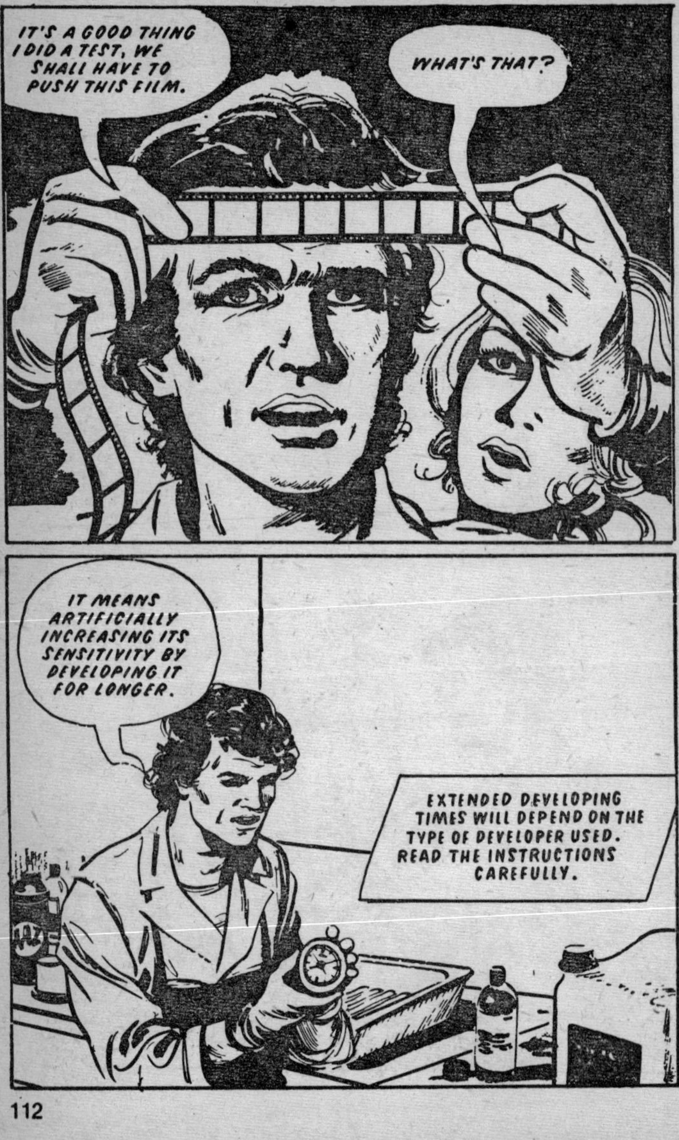

Now on to colour

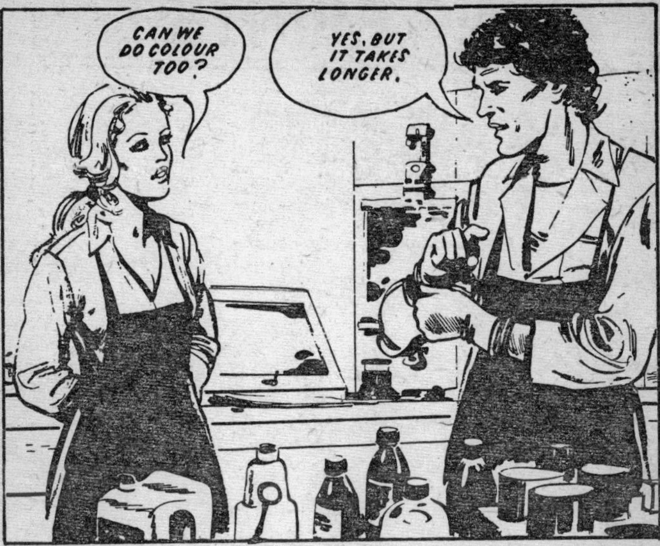

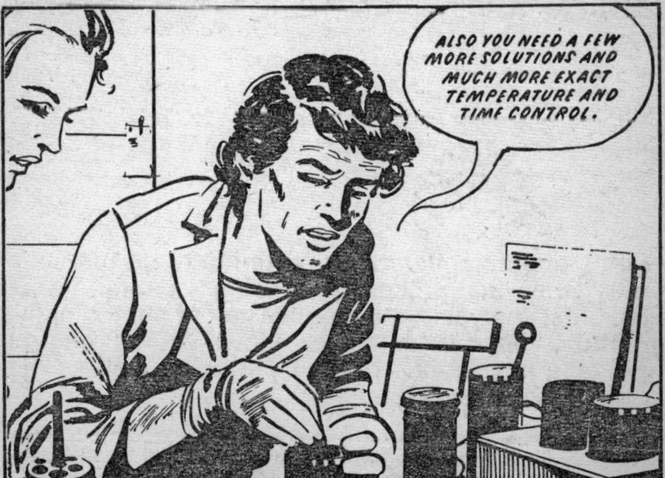

Chapter 14

MAKING PRINTS

Some photographers look on printing not just as a necessary final process in making a photo, but as the most enjoyable and creative part of photography. Printing your own negatives allows you full control over the appearance of your prints, as well as the required size, and cropping.

It is convenient to have a well equipped darkroom but many photographers manage well with temporary darkrooms. Removable blackout can be contrived with hardboard or polythene sheeting. Print washing can be done later in the bathroom or kitchen.

Essential starting equipment

Enlarger and lens: A good cheap model will make perfect prints, provided the enlarging lens is good. Expensive models offer more sophistication, especially for colour control and larger prints, though most types allow colour print making.
Dishes: Start with three, for prints 10 x 8ins maximum size.
Safelight: For monochrome this allows comfortable working in an amber/orange low light level. Colour prints in a drum must be handled in complete darkness up to processing stage.
Accessories: Timer (digital watches are fine), enlarger easel (paper holder), thermometer, print handling tongs.
Paper: In various sizes, surfaces and grades of contrast. Resin-coated (RC) paper is the quickest and easiest to process and dry.
Chemicals: Print developer (not that used for films), rinse water or stop bath, rapid fixer (last two as used for films).

Making a black and white print

1. **Set up enlarger**
   The enlarger allows the chosen negative to be projected to required size and focused sharply. Set lens at a mid-range aperture (say f/8).

2. **Make test strip**
   Expose a small strip of paper for progressive times (2, 4, 8, 16 seconds) and process it (see steps 4-6). Judge which looks best. If all too dark or light, make further tests at shorter or longer times.

3. **Expose the print**
   Put the sheet of printing paper on the enlarger easel and expose for correct test time.

4. **Develop**
   Rock dish throughout. RC paper needs 1 minute, normal papers 2 minutes.

5. **Rinse**
   In water or stop bath. 15 seconds is sufficient.

6. **Fix**
   For 1 minute with rapid fixer and RC paper.

7. **Wash**
   RC paper needs only 4 minutes, conventional (non resin-coated) paper 30/45 minutes. Special print washers ensure proper washing, but not essential.

8. **Dry**
   Lay flat, pin up, or dry in special dryers. RC papers dry rapidly and completely flat.

What you need for printing

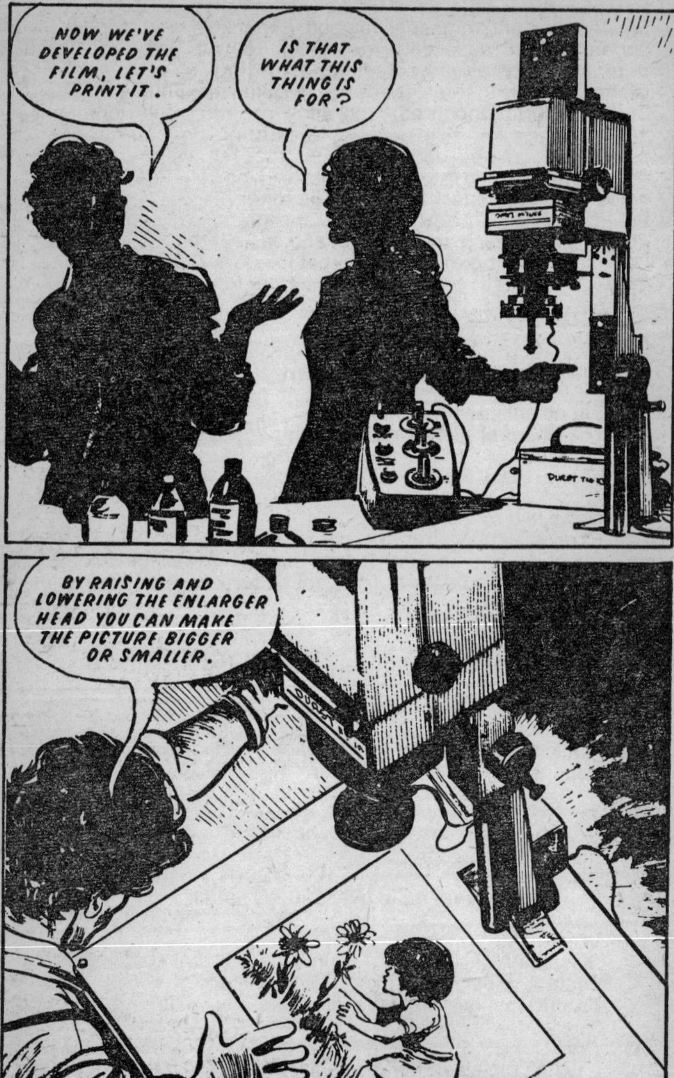

The enlarger

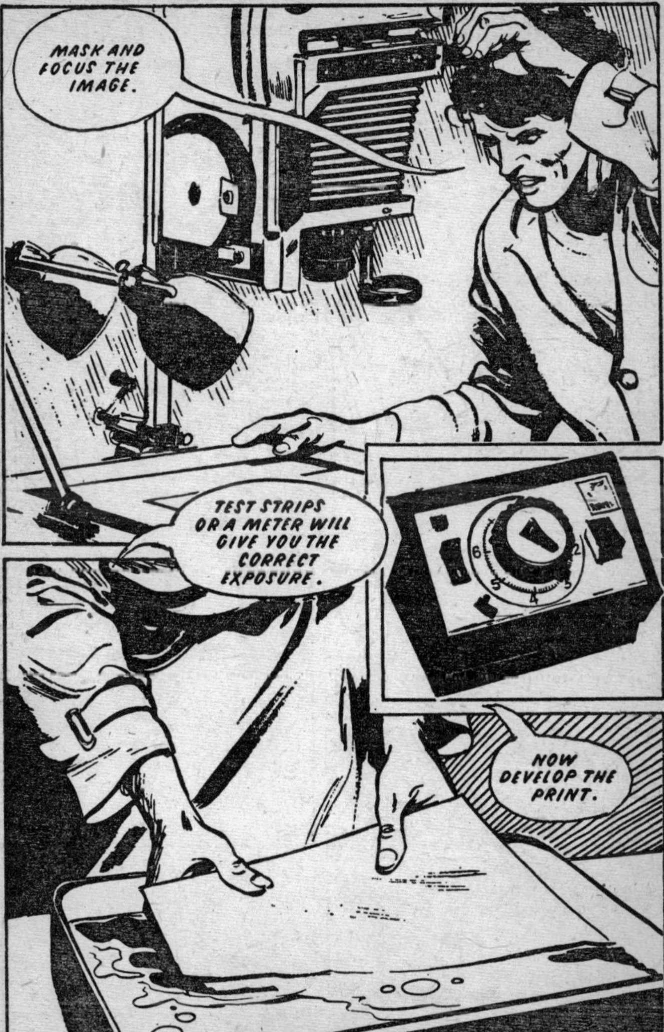

Developing the print

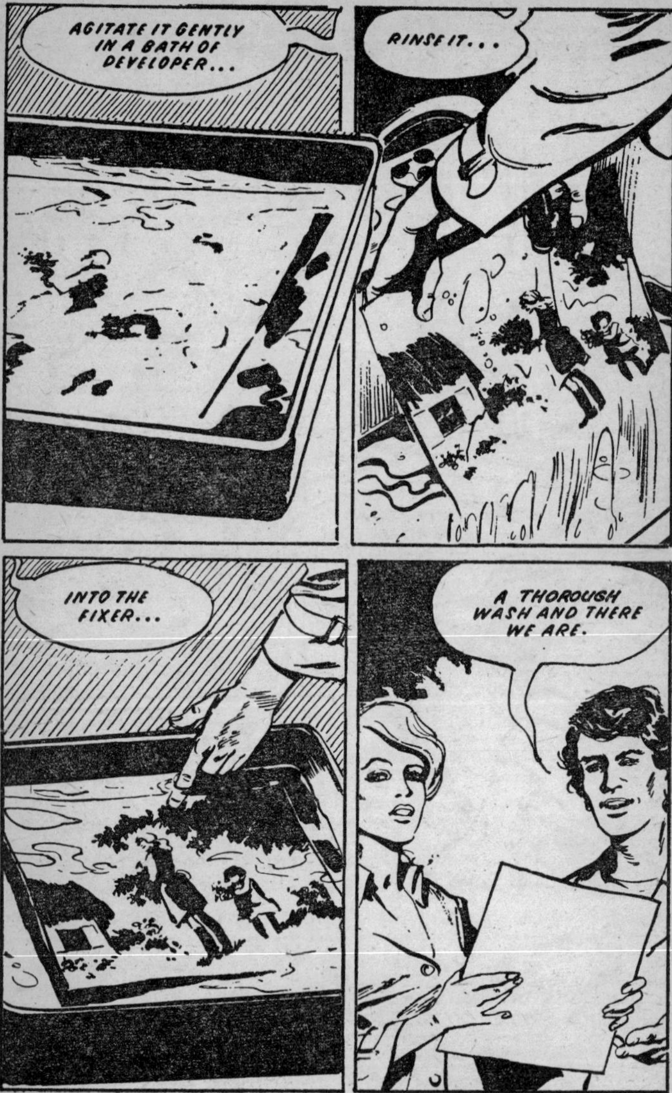

Chapter 15

SOMETHING TO SHOW

Taking lots of photographs is the best way to master photography. As you can see, there is no great mystique behind photography. It's a matter of learning, step by step, how to use the camera's controls to make the sort of photograph you want.

Be selective

Some photographs you will consider failures, but they are not a waste of time, if you learn something from each shot before putting it aside. Study your not-bad and quite-good pictures too. Try to see what you should have done to make them better, or what it is that makes them appealing.

This deduction-selection process is vital, if you want to become a competent photographer. It starts, of course, when you first look through the viewfinder. Be selective too, as you examine contact-sheet proofs or small prints, to decide which are worth enlarging, and what changes need to be made at this stage. Cropping, trimming a picture down to the essential minimum size and enlarging that area, can make a vast improvement.

Showing with style

A little showmanship goes a long way in helping you and others appreciate your photography. Select the best photos and arrange them in albums and perhaps with informative captions. Don't follow a strictly chronological sequence. Try to group photos which look well together, arranging them by subject or perhaps in contrast one with another as a running picture story. Think like this for a slide showing: don't show lots of slides of the same thing. Leave people wishing there were more; a ten minute show is long enough.

A pin board in the kitchen can make an entertaining and ever changing display of your snaps or best prints.

Widen your photo interests

Broaden your photo-horizons by looking through photo-magazines and books. Visit photo-exhibitions, and look at photographs other than those you usually take — perhaps they'll give you a new angle on photography.

Photographic competitions are fun and a great incentive to help you to organize your photographs by giving you a theme. They can be profitable too. Photo clubs run competitons and exhibitions, and are often helpful in technical matters.

Display your prints

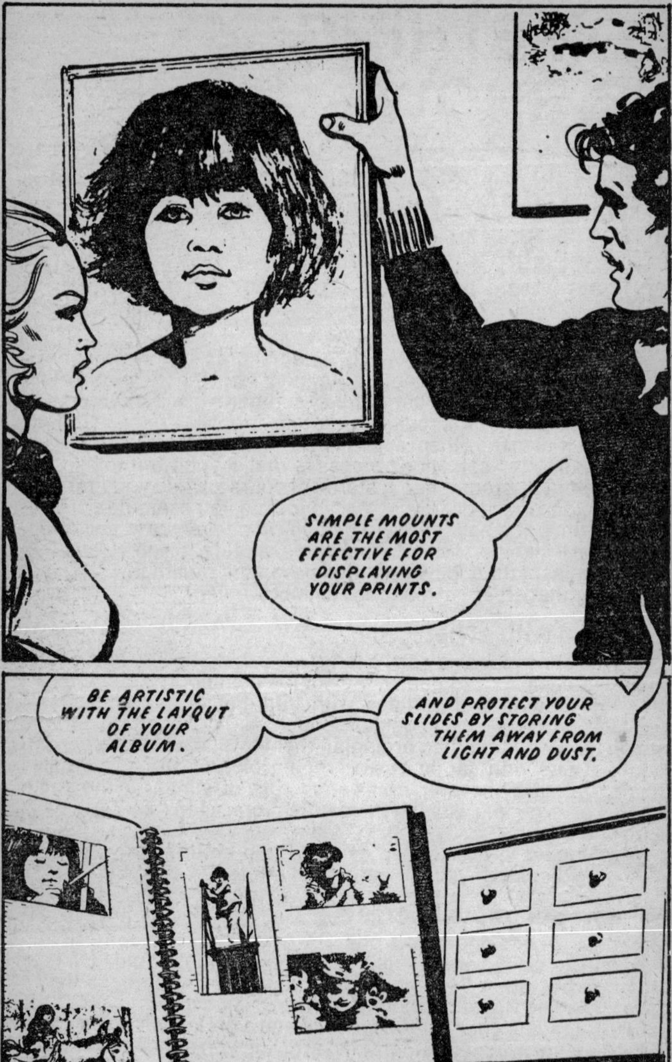

Test your lenses

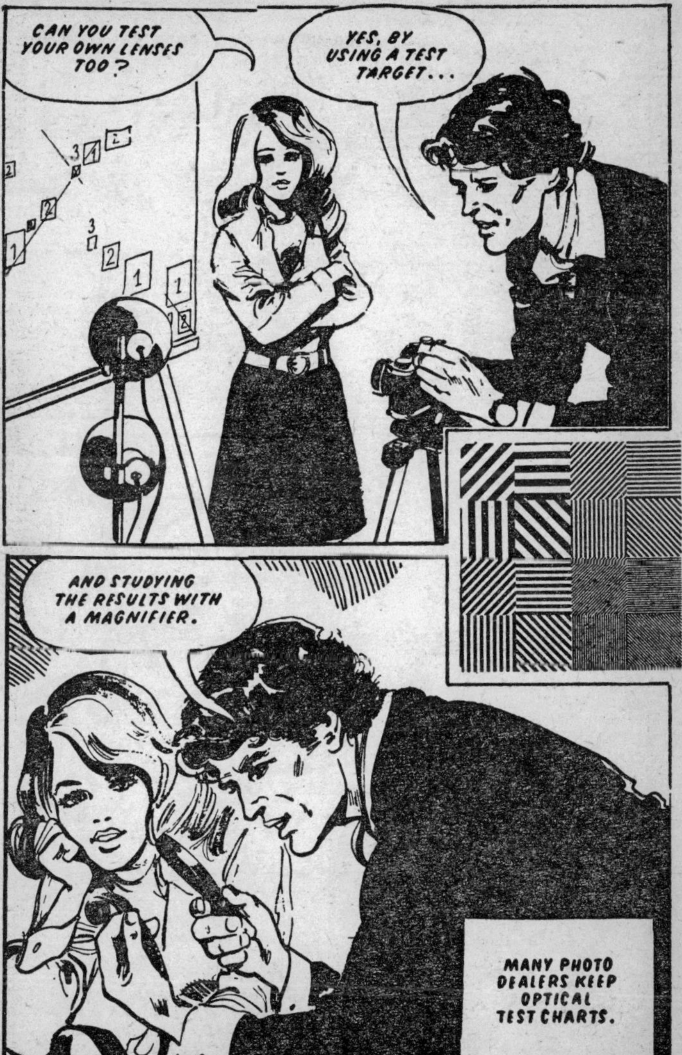

Projection pleasures

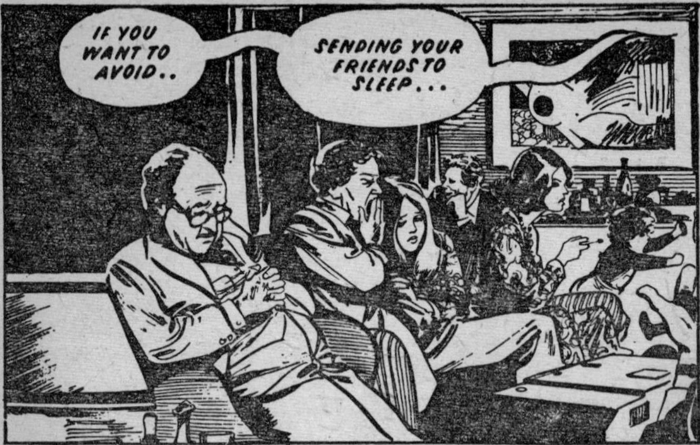

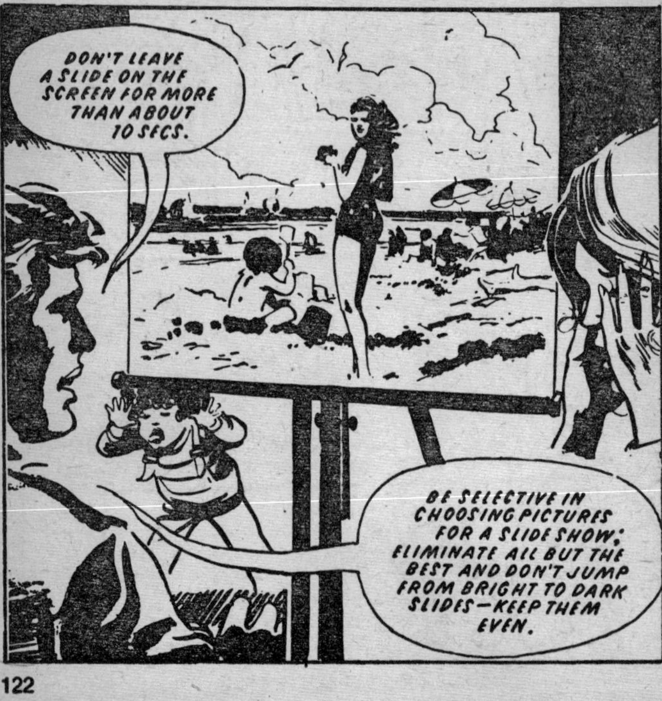

Lessons from lost shots

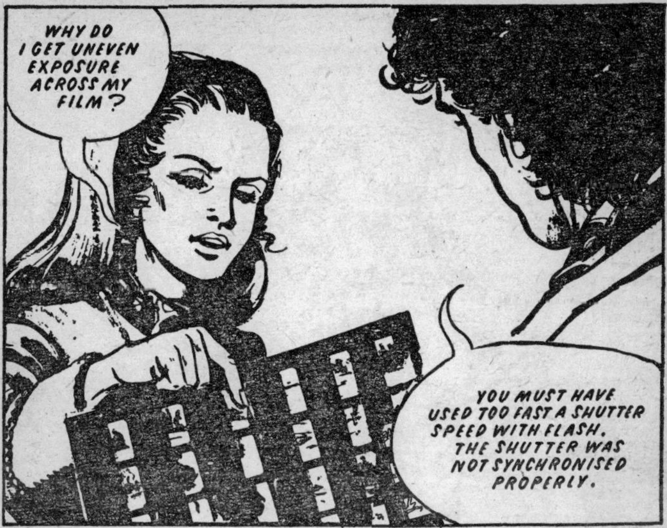

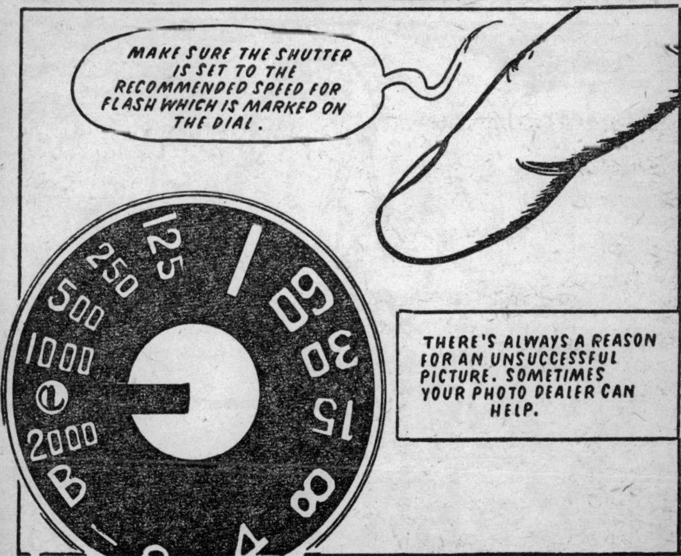

What lies ahead?

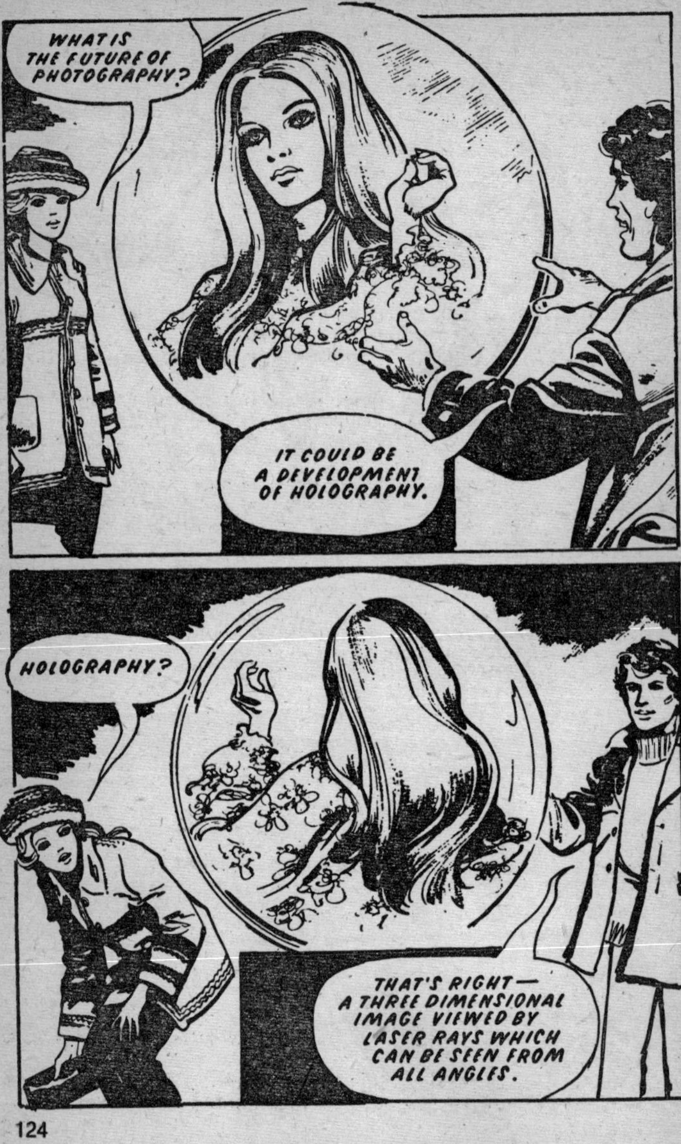

GLOSSARY

ASA: System for measuring a film's sensitivity to light. Films for normal use vary between 50 and 400ASA.
Air release: Pneumatic device for triggering a camera shutter by remote control.
Aperture: Variable-sized opening in the iris diaphragm of a camera. Calibrated in f-stop numbers, e.g. f/5.6, f/8, f/16, etc.
Cable release: Remote control shutter release device, often used to avoid camera shake (qv).
Cartridge: Light-tight plastic film container for 110 or 126 films.
Cassette: Light-tight metal film container for 35mm films.
Camera shake: Movement of the camera during exposure that produces overlapping or blurred images.
Colour temperature: Expressed in degrees Kelvin. A glowing body like the filament of a lamp becomes more blue and less red the hotter it gets and vice versa. Daylight colour films are formulated to match the bluish light of diffused noonday sun. Type A films are for the more reddish light of photofloods.
Colour reversal film: A film which produces a positive colour transparency (slide) by direct processing.
Contre jour, or against-the-light: A technique of taking a photograph with the subject between the camera and the main source of light — usually the sun.
Compact camera: Usually takes 35mm film but does not normally have through-the-lens view finding or interchangeable lenses.
Daylight film: Colour film made to give good colour rendering by noonday light or flash.
Depth of field: Range of distances from the lens, at any given setting, within which everything is in focus.
Diaphragm: Thin metal leaves within the lens, which overlap to make variable-sized apertures (qv); often called the iris diaphragm.
Distribution board: Electric switch unit usually containing two or more 13 amp sockets and a switch for half or full power for photofloods.
DIN: German film rating system.
Electric eye sensor: Built in light meter, which controls exposure automatically.
Electronic flash: Flash produced by an electric discharge through a tube filled with gas (usually xenon) under reduced pressure.

Exposure: Setting of the iris diaphragm and the shutter to control the amount of light that reaches the film.
Exposure meter or light meter: Light sensitive device for determining exposure.
f-stop numbers: Numbers on a lens indicating apertures available. the smaller the number the larger the aperture.
Field of view: Effective picture area given by any particular lens. On a 35mm SLR (qv) camera the standard 50mm lens covers a field of view of about 48 degrees.
Filters: Coloured or treated glass or gelatine placed over the front of the lens to correct colour rendering or for special effects.
Fixed focus: A camera with no focus adjustment.
Flare: Fog or degraded image on a photograph caused by light reflecting from inside the camera or the surface of the lens onto the film.
Flash bulb: A glass bulb containing highly inflammable material, which produces a brilliant, momentary light when contacted by an electric current.
Flash cube: Four miniature flash bulbs in a rotatable plastic case.
Flash synchronisation: Means of ensuring that the flash and shutter opening take place simultaneously.
Focal length: Distance from the optical centre of the lens to the point at which an image is focused with a lens set at infinity. Usually measured in millimetres. A lens is described as wide angle (35mm and less on a 35mm camera), standard (40-55mm) and long focus or telephoto (85mm or more).
Fog: Unintentional exposure of film to light, usually caused by loading in bright sunlight, or leakage of light into the camera.
Fill-in: Light from a secondary source, used to ensure that there is detail in shadows, or to reduce contrast.
Gel: Coloured plastic material used for altering the quality of artificial lighting.
Guide numbers (GN): Means of describing the power of a flashgun, with film of any given ASA (qv). Guide numbers are usually given in feet and meters. Dividing the guide number by the aperture in use will give the correct flash-to-subject distance. Alternatively, dividing the GN by the distance will give the aperture to use.
High key: Describes a photograph in which nearly all the tones are very light grey to white.
Low key: Describes a photograph in which nearly all the tones are dark grey to black. Opposite of high key.
Magicube: Similar to flashcube (qv), but mechanically fired. Can only be used with cameras designed for it.
Main light: Sun or other light used to define the subject and control contrast and modelling of the subject.
Masking: A dye in colour negative film to improve colour rendering. Masked negatives have a strong orange cast.
Negative: Colour or black-and-white film which gives reversed values of colour, light and shade. Any number of prints can be made from the negative.
Open flash: Use of flash without synchronisation (qv). The shutter is set at Time or Bulb, the flash fired manually, and the shutter closed again manually.

Over exposure: Too much light reaching the film, resulting in a dense negative, or thin transparency.
Parallax: The difference between the view in the viewfinder and the view seen by the lens. Specially noticeable in close-up shots. Does not occur with SLR cameras (qv).
Portrait lens or attachment: Placed on the front of a lens, it makes possible head and shoulders shots with cameras that do not normally focus closely enough.
Photoflood: An over-run electric bulb, giving a high output. The No 1 size burns at about 275 watts, giving light equivalent to about six 100w bulbs. Available in bayonet or screw fitttings.
Rangefinder: Optical device for measuring the camera-to-subject distance.
Reflector: Usually a white or silvered card, used for reflecting light into shadows.
Shutter: Device for determining the duration of an exposure. Can be of two types. The focal plane shutter is a moveable blind travelling across in front of the film. A variable-sized slit in the blind gives variable exposure. The between-the-lens shutter is like an instant return iris diaphragm (qv).
SLR, or single lens reflex camera: A camera with which the exact scene to be photographed can be seen through the taking lens by means of a mirror and pentaprism. An SLR also takes interchangeable lenses.
Synchro-sunlight: Synchronised flash (qv) used outdoors as a fill-in (qv) to reduce contrast in bright sunlight.
Slave unit: A device which fires a remote flashgun, when it receives light from a flashgun fired by the camera.
Slide: A transparency (qv) mounted for projection. The mount for a 35mm, 110 or 126 transparency is 2 x 2ins.
Soft focus: An image artificially softened, not simply out of focus.
Telephoto lens: Used for distant subjects, or where a restricted field of view (qv) is needed, as in portraits. Telephotos are of 85mm or more focal length (qv) on 35mm cameras.
Transparency: A positive image produced on colour reversal film, which has to be projected or viewed by transmitted light.
Tripod: Used for supporting a camera, usually consists of three telescopic legs and a universally adjustable head for mounting the camera.
Type A film: Colour film made to give good colour rendering for photoflood light.
Umbrella flash: White or silver umbrella used as a reflector bouncing the light of a flashgun.
Under exposure: When insufficient light has reached the film, resulting in dense transparencies or thin negatives.
UV, ultra violet: A UV filter helps to overcome excessive blue in sky at high altitudes, or warm up shadows on a sunny day, especially by the sea. A UV filter is also used as a means of protecting the front element of the lens.
Wide angle lens: A lens giving a wide field of view, which also makes things look a long way away. Popular lengths with a 35mm camera are 35mm, 28mm, 24mm and 18mm, with corresponding angles of view of 63°, 75°, 84° and 100°.
Zoom lens: Lens of variable focal length (qv).